Neighborhood Democracy

Neighborhood Democracy

The Politics and Impacts of Decentralization

Douglas Yates
Yale University

Lexington Books
D.C. Heath and Company
Lexington, Massachusetts
Toronto London

Library of Congress Cataloging in Publication Data

Yates, Douglas, 1944-
Neighborhood democracy.

Bibliography: p.
1. Decentralization in government–United States. 2. Municipal government–United States. 3. Community power. I. Title.
JS341.Y37 320.4 73-7732
ISBN 0-669-89334-X

Published simultaneously in Canada.

Printed in the United States of America.

International Standard Book Number: 0-669-89334-X

Library of Congress Catalog Card Number: 73-7732

To my Mother and Father
who taught me the value
of the small community.

Contents

List of Figures

List of Tables

Preface

This study examines the politics and impacts of decentralization experiments in urban government. It attempts to evaluate the experience of decentralization and to explain why certain experiments succeed and others fail. In the course of the study four hypotheses about decentralization are tested: (1) Does decentralization make government more responsive and have an impact on neighborhood problems; (2) Does it strengthen representation and internal democracy; (3) Does it produce strong political leadership in the neighborhood; and (4) Does it reduce feelings of powerlessness and alienation from government? The first three chapters deal with the "problem of decentralization" in an urban context. The first charts the rise of current demands for decentralization, the second explores the historical background of neighborhood government, and the third analyzes the concept of decentralization and distinguishes different forms of decentralization. The next three chapters report the author's research on seven experiments in decentralization in two cities: New York and New Haven. Chapter 4 deals with initiatives and impacts, Chapter 5 with representation and internal democracy. In both chapters, the record of the experiments is judged in terms of a number of common tests that permit a comparative analysis of the decentralization experience. Chapter 6 identifies four different styles of neighborhood leadership, examines the political implications of the different styles, and shows how the structure of the experiments shapes leadership style. The last four chapters attempt to explain the evidence presented in the previous three. Chapter 7 examines the "political economy of decentralization" and ends with a structural explanation of the impact of decentralization. Chapter 8 examines the view from city hall and shows how certain weaknesses in decentralization experiments can be explained in terms of city hall's problems in "making decentralization work." Chapter 9 examines patterns of popular support for and opposition to decentralization and shows that the future of neighborhood government is limited by conflicting, often contradictory public beliefs. Chapter 10 presents and justifies a strategy of "unbalanced growth" and shows how decentralization fits into a broader context of development and democracy.

Acknowledgments

Writing a first book is like running a long-distance race over a totally unfamiliar course. You are not sure where you are going, but you are quite sure you are not going to get there. And when you are finished, it is hard to extract a sense of satisfaction from feelings of physical relief and mild incredulity that the enterprise was undertaken in the first place. But, there is also a fundamental difference: the runner works alone, the first-time author depends at every step on the counsel, assistance, and support of friends, family, and academic colleagues.

This project grew out of research I began at the New York City Rand Institute in 1970. Robert Yin of Rand got me interested in neighborhood government that summer and has continued to guide and improve my work ever since. This manuscript was originally prepared as a dissertation in the Department of Political Science at Yale. My advisor was James Fesler, and his clarity of mind, experience, and common sense have been invaluable to me throughout my research and writing. Other present and former members of the Yale Department who offered help and criticism at various stages were David Mayhew, James David Barber, Robert Dahl, and Willis Hawley. Also, John Perry Miller, Director of the Institution of Social and Policy Studies at Yale, nudged me forward at the same time that he provided a congenial institutional setting for research and teaching.

In the course of doing research, many people opened their doors and their files and listened to my questions and ideas. Among these, I am particularly indebted to Robert Mitchell, Lewis Feldstein, James Oesterle, and Buz Williams in New York City's Office of Neighborhood Government. Andrew Houlding of the New Haven Journal Courier and Steven Weisman of the New York Times gave me valuable background information and time-saving access to newspaper files. I am also deeply grateful to four patient and able women who helped prepare the manuscript and encouraged its author through several revisions: Becky Whitehead, Marilyn Satterthwaite, Julie Merkt, and Sharon Hornberger.

In the final analysis, the most important debts are incurred closer to home. Most of what I have—especially my education and the opportunity to grow up a city boy—I owe to my parents. Finally, my wife, Doris, has been a constant source of warmth, understanding, and keen editorial judgment. With this much support and assistance, it should be clear that the shortcomings of this book can only be attributed to the author's "invincible ignorance."

Part I
The Problem of Decentralization

1 Decentralization in Urban Politics

Decentralization is a fighting word in many American cities. Advocates claim decentralization will bring government closer to the people and revitalize urban neighborhoods—especially poor, black ones. Opponents see decentralization as a betrayal of integration and the merit system in urban governments. Some argue that decentralization will produce racism and arbitrary rule. In recent years, the decentralization debate has produced not only public controversy but also important innovations in urban government.[1]

Academic writing on decentralization has followed the lines of the public debate. Some writers, like Milton Kotler, simply argue the case for decentralization and present a blueprint for neighborhood government.[2] Other writers, like Alan Altshuler, examine the claims for and against decentralization.[3] The question they ask is whether decentralization is a good or bad thing. Much has also been written on the case that first drew widespread attention to the politics of decentralization: the Ocean Hill-Brownsville school experiment in New York City.[4] Recently, several case studies on other decentralization experiments have appeared.[5]

What has been lacking in the public debate and in academic writings is a systematic examination of decentralization based on a comparative analysis of existing experiments. This study attempts to contribute such a perspective. Three problems are raised. The first is analytical: what does "decentralization" mean? The second is empirical: what is the experience of decentralization in American cities—both in the past and in current experiments? The third is theoretical: what are the implications of decentralization for political development and democratic theory?

As a preliminary definition, we will say decentralization means the delegation of administrative and/or political power from the city government to neighborhood units. The term "neighborhood government" is often used as a synonym for decentralization. "Community control" means the devolution of dominant power to neighborhood units. Understood in this way, the concept of decentralization extends beyond administrative organization. It raises questions of citizen participation and democratic control of government; of responsiveness and accountability in government.

The Rise of Decentralization

There are several reasons why demands for decentralization arise in urban politics. They include:

1. *The Failure of Integration.* In the 1960s, civil rights activists fought to integrate schools, neighborhoods, and other public facilities. But in many cities, the demands for integration changed to demands for community control when promises of integration went unfulfilled. In New York City, for example, the community control movement dates back to the opening of an intermediate school in Harlem in 1966. Promised an integrated school, Harlem parents and residents sought community control when it became clear that I.S. 201 would be segregated.[6]

2. *The Effects of Protest and Community Action.* The civil rights struggle spilled over into neighborhood protest when residents organized to improve housing, education, and government services.[7] Later, neighborhood protest was extended and institutionalized by the community action program of the War on Poverty.[8] The result was what Daniel Bell has called the "community revolution":[9] the creation of entrenched organizations demanding increased citizen participation and greater government responsiveness to neighborhood problems. In the late 1960s, protests also developed in white neighborhoods. Charging that their neighborhoods were ignored by city hall, white protesters demanded improved services and a greater say in government.

The charge that city government had grown remote and unresponsive was thus strongly articulated by neighborhood protesters, but its source lay in the changing character of urban political institutions—and especially in the decline of the machine and the weakness of representative structures.

3. *The Decline of the Machine.* The old time political machine has declined or disappeared in most cities. As a result, party structures no longer play a powerful role in channeling and aggregating citizen demands.

4. *The Weakness of Representative Structures.* At the same time, city councils are weakly developed as representative, interest-articulating bodies.[10] City councilmen are typically understaffed and underpaid, if they are paid at all. In many cities, councilmen serve on a part-time basis. Representation is further undermined in cities with at-large elections.[11] In addition, the urban political process is confused by overlapping systems of representation and by cross-cutting constituencies. Who does the neighborhood resident turn to for help: his councilman, state assemblyman, state senator, congressman or senator?

Given intense citizen demands for representation and responsiveness and weak representative linkages between citizens and city government, citizens often feel they must "fight city hall" directly if they wish to have any effect. But the mayors of most cities in the late 1960s would have had difficulty responding to neighborhood demands even if they had wanted to. Two basic features of urban government militated against responsiveness to neighborhood problems: centralization and fragmentation.

5. *Government Centralization.* The decentralization movement arose in large part as a reaction against the progressive centralization of urban government. Strong mayor charters were an early centralizing force. Increased spending for

local services led to expanded bureaucracies in the school system and in other departments. In the 1950s, the urban renewal program generated centralized redevelopment agencies at the local level. The rise of strong public service unions added further to the concentration of power.

This study focuses on New York and New Haven, and it is no accident that the era of the fifties and early sixties was the era of Robert Moses and Richard C. Lee—master builders, perhaps; centralists, without question.[12]

6. *Government Fragmentation.* Before the rise of the decentralization movement, city government was not only centralized; it was also fragmented. In most cities, considerable power resided in independent boards and commissions which, from the neighborhood perspective, were no less a part of centralized, "downtown" government than city hall. At the same time, the diversity of boards and commissions added to the complexity and confusion of government. From the city hall perspective, fragmentation meant that the mayor often could not satisfy neighborhood demands because he did not control the relevant decisions or decisionmakers.

7. *The Nature of Urban Public Services.* In addition to the various centralizing forces, one centrifugal force also existed in city government that gave impetus to the decentralization movement. That centrifugal force was found in the very nature of urban public services.

Urban governments provide daily services that have a direct and visible effect on people's lives: services like garbage collection, fire and police protection, sewer and park maintenance, and public education. The most obvious characteristic of these services is that their delivery and impact are locality-specific and highly divisible for that reason. Garbage collection is not an indivisible public good like national defense. Citizens do not care how well the city is collecting garbage, in general, but whether garbage is being collected on their block. The same is true for police protection, public education, and street-paving. The extreme case of indivisibility occurs when a service affects everyone in the same way. The extreme case of divisibility occurs when everyone is affected by a service differently.[13] My assertion is that many urban services are highly divisible.

Furthermore, public services differ not only in divisibility but also in variation in individual need. For example, citizens have the same need for national defense. By contrast, bridges and parks, which like national defense are relatively indivisible public goods, serve individuals with very different needs. Postal services may be divisible—may vary dramatically from place to place—but most individuals have the same need: to have their mail delivered. By contrast, urban services like garbage, and fire and police protection are not only highly divisible in their allocation, but also are delivered to individuals with very different needs.[14] (See Figure 1-1.)

If this is true, urban service delivery takes place in a highly decentralized market in which consumers with different needs seek many different kinds of

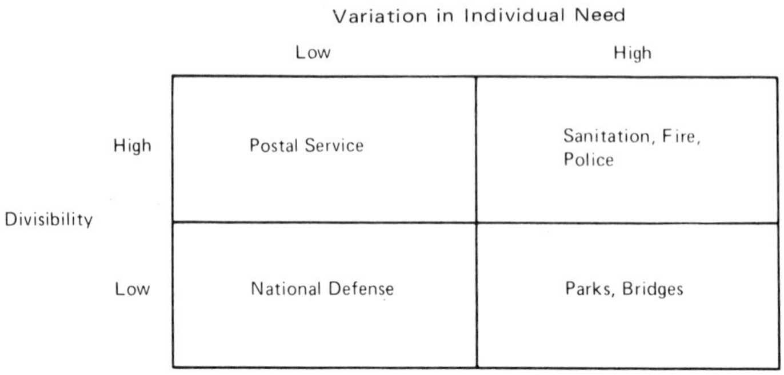

Figure 1-1. A Logic of Public Goods and Services: Service Divisibility and Variation in Need.

goods and services. Given the number of different park benches, garbage cans, catch basins, traffic lights, or abandoned buildings in any city, many demands inevitably arise that cannot easily be aggregated by existing broad-based interest groups or solved by a generalized government response.

Thus, my argument is that urban public services are intrinsically fragmented and that this fragmentation puts centrifugal pressure on service delivery. The characteristics of urban public employees reinforce this fragmentation. As James Q. Wilson has pointed out, discretion in the police department is greatest at the bottom of the hierarchy.[15] Police policy is what the patrolman on the beat decides to do or not to do in specific encounters with citizens. And according to Michael Lipsky, the same patterns apply to other "street-level bureaucrats," such as teachers and judges.[16]

The Problem of Urban Democracy

In the broadest sense, decentralization is a response to the belief that urban government has failed—that it has not fulfilled its promise of relatively direct democracy. Direct democracy depends on proximity and participation. In the New England Town Meeting, each individual represented himself in an easily accessible community forum. As one moves away from this ideal type, government becomes less proximate, and self-representation gives way to representation by elected officials with larger and larger constituencies. The central problem in urban democracy is that its proximity does not lead to strong citizen participation. This problem is presented schematically in Figure 1-2, where proximity is defined in terms of (a) the citizen's physical distance from government and (b) a scale of representativeness expressed as the ratio of leaders to citizens in different constituencies. Participation is measured by election

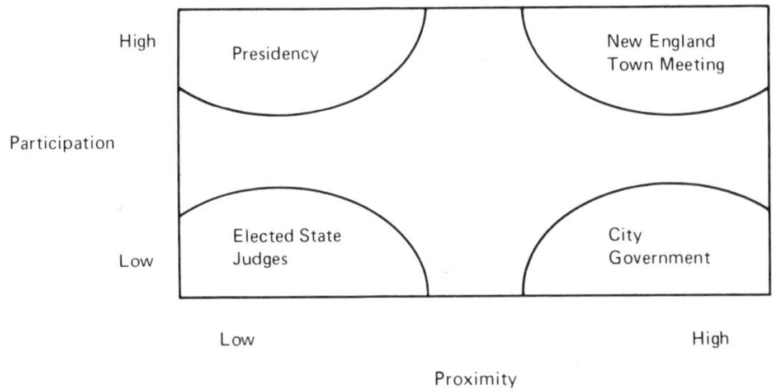

Figure 1-2. Proximity and Participation in Political Systems.

turnout.[17] Given this result, advocates claim that decentralization to neighborhood units will close the gap between proximity and participation, and thereby fulfill the city's potential for responsive and democratic government.

The Politics and Impacts of Decentralization

In what follows, we will test several hypotheses about the politics and impacts of decentralization. The first hypothesis is that decentralization will develop an indigenous political leadership in urban neighborhoods.[18] This hypothesis entails several more specific questions. What kinds of people become neighborhood leaders? What are their leadership styles and political attitudes?

A second hypothesis is that decentralization will diminish feelings of powerlessness. The claim is that decentralization, particularly in the form of community control, will increase the local citizen's sense of political efficacy—his belief that he has a voice in government and that his voice is being heard.[19]

A third hypothesis is that decentralization will increase representation and accountability. It is also claimed that neighborhood institutions will bring democratic procedures and decisionmaking to street-level politics.[20]

The fourth hypothesis is that by bringing government "closer to the people," decentralization will make government more responsive. The weak form of this claim is that government services will be more efficient and better fitted to neighborhood needs. In its strong form, the claim is that decentralized government will bring about "social change" by solving neighborhood problems.[21]

Having examined these hypotheses, we will attempt to explain the patterns that emerge. To the extent that decentralization experiments do not fulfill these hopeful hypotheses, explanations will be sought in obstacles to decentralization—both at the community level and in city government. At the community level, we will examine the costs of decentralization in time, community conflict, and conflict with city hall to see how much these obstacles reduce the impact of decentralization. At the city hall level, we will examine government conflict, citizen-bureaucrat conflict, and general political conflict to see how much these problems limit city government's ability to "make decentralization work."

We will also ask what kind of support exists for neighborhood government to see if opposition is such as to limit the political viability of decentralization.

Further we will seek to relate the experience of decentralization to larger issues of political development and democratic theory. With respect to political development we ask the following questions: Under what conditions will decentralization have the greatest impact? What urban problems are most amenable to solution through decentralization strategies? What conflicts and trade-offs exist between different goals of political development? What are the alternative futures of decentralization? And what implications do theories of political development have for decentralization experiments?

With respect to democratic theory we ask: What happens to minority interests in decentralized government? Does decentralized government mean political fragmentation, and, if so, what are the implications for democracy in the larger society? What is the relationship between size and democracy in neighborhood experiments? What are the implications of decentralization for participation and polyarchy—the control of leaders by nonleaders?

Finally, existing experiments differ in fundamental ways, and we wish to see what difference these structural differences make in the politics and impacts of decentralization. The question for public policy is what kind of decentralization produces what kind of result?

The Nature of the Research

The study examines seven experiments in two cities: New York and New Haven. Decentralization experiments in other cities have been investigated in less depth, and studies of other existing experiments have been consulted. The seven experiments provide a wide spectrum of structure and function. They are: block associations, community task forces, community boards, and community school boards in New York; neighborhood corporations, Model Cities, and the Hill Health Corporation in New Haven. Research on these experiments includes 85 long interviews with the leaders of the organizations as well as an analysis of minutes of meetings, file documents, and newspaper records. In other parts of the study, findings are reported from a survey of 450 New York residents in three neighborhoods concerning service delivery and attitudes toward neighborhood government. For the discussion of governmental responses to decentralization, interviews were conducted with sixty district-level public employees in New York and with twenty city officials involved in decentralization experiments in New York and New Haven. For the discussion of the question "who wants neighborhood government and in what form," an analysis was made of an unusual file of public documents. In 1970, New York's Office of Neighborhood Government held a series of 200 "consultations" with neighborhood residents concerning a proposed plan for neighborhood government. This record constitutes an informal constitutional convention on the questions of whether decentralization should be advanced and, if so, in what form.

2 Power to the Neighborhoods: The Background of an Idea

In the 1969 New York mayoralty campaign, "power to the neighborhoods" was the campaign slogan of an unusual candidate. The candidate was novelist Norman Mailer; and since he claimed to be part visionary and part conservative, it was hard to know whether the slogan looked back to a fondly-remembered past or pointed forward to an imagined future.[1] As it turned out, the idea of "power to the neighborhoods" was not simply the fanciful inspiration of an "educational" campaign. The idea has persisted in New York and in other cities and, in fact, a strong impetus to decentralization could be discerned before 1969.

In 1967, an advisory panel headed by Ford Foundation President McGeorge Bundy produced a blueprint for school decentralization which led to the controversial decentralization experiments in New York City.[2] In 1968 Mayor Kevin White of Boston launched a Little City Halls program, saying that "the greatest domestic crisis in America today is the failure of the cities to respond to the human needs of its citizens."[3] Later, in 1970, Mayor Lindsay announced a "Plan for Neighborhood Government," the goals of which were to improve service delivery and "reduce the alienation and distance that citizens feel toward a remote city government."[4]

More generally, Alan Altshuler writes of a "widespread demand for increased citizen participation in the governance of America's largest cities" and underscores the "black demand for participation."[5] At its 1969 convention, the NAACP adopted a resolution "strongly support(ing) the concept of community control of public schools, particularly in the big-city school systems of North and West, as a means of achieving fundamental changes in the school, and insuring accountability."[6] The Urban League also adopted a community control resolution in 1969; and Whitney Young, the league's director then, commented that "community control is the most crucial issue right now . . . (I)nstitutions have failed because control isn't in the hands of people who live in the communities."[7]

After the Bundy panel, other "blue-ribbon" task forces recommended decentralization. The Advisory Commission on Intergovernmental Relations urged that "neighborhood initiative and self-respect be fostered by authorizing counties and large cities to establish neighborhood subunits endowed with limited powers of taxation and local self-government."[8] The Kerner Commission (National Advisory Commission on Civil Disorders) urged the development of neighborhood action task forces;[9] while the Douglas Commission (National

Commission on Urban Problems) recommended the "decentralization of municipal services to neighborhood city halls."[10] The Bar Association of New York City concluded a study of urban government and service delivery with strong recommendations for decentralization.[11]

In light of these developments, one observer concluded that " 'decentralization' has, in general, become a very fashionable idea."[12] Another determined that " 'decentralization of administration is in the air everywhere'."[13]

Having charted the emergence of the decentralization issue, we return to the question of what precedents, if any, the idea of "power to the neighborhoods" has in American urban history. The argument of this chapter is that neighborhood democracy has few precedents—that decentralization and widespread citizen participation have not been characteristic of American cities in earlier historical periods. It is argued, too, that with the exception of certain Progressive theorists and city planners there has been little intellectual support for decentralization.

This interpretation of urban politics differs from an influential thesis advanced by Herbert Kaufman.[14] His thesis is that urban political institutions follow a cycle produced by a "change in emphasis among three values: representativeness, politically neutral competence, and executive leadership."[15] Kaufman asserts that in the postcolonial period Americans reacted against "executive dominance in the colonial era" and placed a strong emphasis on direct democracy and, by extension, on decentralized government. However, this emphasis led to the excesses of machine control and corruption. The reaction, according to Kaufman, was the Progressives' drive for politically neutral competence. Their efforts were to "take administration out of politics by lodging it in independent branches and commissions and by introducing the merit system to break the hold of party in bureaucracies."[16] In Kaufman's theory, the excess implicit in this reaction was a fragmentation of government that "reduced both efficiency and representativeness." Hence, there was a further reaction: a "search for unification" leading to demands for increased executive power.

According to this analysis, the decentralization movement represents another turn of the cycle—another reaction against executive dominance and a demand for greater representativeness in urban government. Although Kaufman's thesis is persuasive in some respects, there is an alternative explanation that yields a totally different interpretation of the nature and status of the decentralization movement. This explanation is that since the colonial era, urban government has been fragmented and that bosses, reformers, and strong mayor advocates alike have sought to harness political power in the city by centralizing it. If this is so, cities have never been decentralized, and the present movement is something new under the sun.

To establish this case, it is necessary first to distinguish between decentralization and fragmentation. Decentralization is a process in which power is devolved vertically from center to locality. In contrast, fragmentation means a horizontal division of powers based on functional rather than geographical distinctions.

Early Urban Institutions

There is a romantic notion that a "golden age" of direct democracy and enlightened democratic theory existed in the formative years of American government. In fact, the early political theorists were never advocates of direct democracy in American cities. Theorists as different as Madison and Jefferson agreed on that point. Madison warned against the tyranny of "arbitrary local majorities" in small constituencies. While generally a decentralist, Jefferson was hostile to cities and their governments. Although he wanted to divide counties into "wards" of five or six square miles each and thereby create "Ward Republics" for the "small and yet numerous and interesting concerns of the neighborhood,"[17] this prescription was not directed at the cities. As Anwar Syed has pointed out, "Jefferson's advocacy of the ward republics is indissolubly connected with small rural communities. The wards were to be small enough so that every citizen could attend the town meeting and 'act in person'."[18] Clearly a Jeffersonian ward republic of five square miles located in an urban setting would not have these characteristics. Also, Jefferson believed that urban "mobs" were likely to "add just as much to the support of pure government as sores do to the strength of the human body."[19]

More important, neighborhood democracy was not a feature of government in colonial and postcolonial cities. The political structure of colonial cities is outlined in Ernest Griffith's standard history of American city government.[20] While noting that democratic self-government was a characteristic of many towns, and especially New England towns, Griffith emphasizes that politics in incorporated municipalities was a different matter. One-third of the twenty-four cities incorporated in the colonial period had charters as "close" corporations, in which voting membership extended only to city officials and their chosen successors.[21] In the sixteen more democratic municipalities, participation was usually limited by property qualifications. Such balloting as existed was highly informal—"often in open meeting or nonsecret."[22] In general, participation in the "few vigorously contested elections" was low:

> In Boston in 1733 the maximum vote cast on the hotly disputed question of establishing a public market was 805 out of a total population of 16,000—a total of about 5 percent or perhaps 20 percent of the adult males. In general, for its representatives to the general court the vote in Boston was but 3 to 4 percent of the population, although 16 percent were probably eligible.[23]

In New Haven in 1766, "only 275 'voters' attended a very important meeting—about 4 percent of the population (or only 16 percent approximately of the adult males). In New York City in 1699 there were 632 votes cast at an election in the assembly . . . indicating 7½ percent of the inhabitants or 30 percent of the adult males participating."[24]

Three other characteristics of early urban government are relevant. First, the governing councils were composed of "wealthy, leading citizens." Second, even in colonial times, there is evidence of a fragmentation of governmental powers among various boards and commissions. Third, there is little evidence of neighborhood-based political organization along ward lines. According to Griffith, "only in New York, Perth Amboy, and New Brunswick does there appear to have been any very considerable development of the ward system. . . ."[25] Thus, in the colonial era, the business of city government was conducted by a small group of leading citizens in a centralized, city-wide forum.

As city government developed in the early nineteenth century, many of these patterns persisted, several new ones appeared, and some changes occurred (for example, the growth of the ward system). Among the most important patterns emerging between 1775 and 1870 were: (1) the further fragmentation of government through the separation of powers and (2) increased state control of local government. Griffith notes that the separation of powers created "a situation of divided and uncertain responsibility" which was made even more confusing by the long ballot, by the "ridiculous extent to which the confidence in popular sovereignty placed the choice of one after another petty administrative official in the hands of the people."[26] Thus, the emphasis on popular sovereignty led to just as much governmental fragmentation as did the emphasis on "nonpartisan competence" in a later era. At the same time, city councils deteriorated as the only representative bodies in urban government "due to the fact that there was no direct compensation for the greatly increased services demanded of the council committees."[27]

The American city that confronted the architects of the great political machines was deeply fragmented and was rapidly relinquishing the powers of self-government to state legislatures. According to one observer of New York, writing in 1866:

> Perhaps the best way of beginning an investigation of the city government would be to go down to the City Hall and look at it. It proved not to be there . . . (I)t has been gradually cut to pieces and scattered over the island . . . Was there ever such a hodgepodge of government before in the world?[28]

At this time, the only strong evidence of neighborhood decentralization was found in the delivery of certain services. In many cities, neighborhood property owners were responsible for streetpaving, and police precincts were frequently controlled by local politicians. Also volunteer, neighborhood-based fire departments were widespread.

The Machine as a Centralizing Force

The machine politicians saw their opportunities and "took 'em,"[29] by centralizing political power. It is a myth that the machine was an early experiment in participatory, neighborhood-based democracy. The most famous machine, Tammany Hall, revealed its undemocratic centralizing methods even before Tweed and his successors came to power. Theoretically, ward committees controlled Tammany Hall. But, in fact, as Jerome Mushkat has shown, "the Hall adopted a more cold-blooded, undemocratic stance, making a fetish out of party unity. The General Committee believed in bickering behind closed doors, then publicly presenting closed, well-drilled ranks instructed through party newspapers . . . Behind all of Tammany's egalitarian pretensions, then, a relatively small group of men met in private caucus and set policy. In defending the system, the Hall always insisted that the caucus, rather than being a closed system, was an instrument of majoritarian rule needed by the unorganized masses to frustrate a moneyed and landed aristocracy."[30] In its full flowering, the machine was a triumph of centralized power and also, as Mandelbaum suggests, of centralized communications.[31] The very idea of a boss or of bossism implies autocratic or nearly autocratic power. Moreover, the bosses were politically accountable only in rare cases, for the simple reason that few of them held public office.[32]

Robert Merton makes the central point in "The Latent Functions of the Machine": "the key structural function of the boss is to organize, centralize, and maintain in good working condition 'the scattered fragments of power' which are at present scattered through our political organization."[33]

Thus, the idea of neighborhood democracy was a fiction maintained by the bosses for the sake of machine power. The bosses skillfully and cynically manipulated neighborhood-based organizations and democratic processes, as the following testimony from a court appearance by Tweed indicates:

Q. When you were in office, did the Ring control the elections in this city at that time?
A. They did, sir; absolutely.
Q. Please tell me what the modus operandi of that was. How did you control the election?
A. Well, each ward had a representative man, who would control matters in his own ward, and whom the various members of the General Committee were to look up to for advice on how to control elections.
Q. The General Committee of Tammany Hall?
A. Of the Regular Organization. . . .
Q. What were they to do, in case you wanted a particular man elected over another?
A. Count the ballots in bulk, or without counting them, announce the result in bulk, or change from one to the other, as the case may have been.
Q. Then these elections were really no elections at all? The ballots were made to bring about any result that you determined beforehand?
A. The ballots made no result; the counters made the result. . . .[34]

At the same time, the machine did provide personal contact with government, pressed citizen complaints against government, and dispersed favors and patronage jobs. So too, some district leaders, such as the Finns and the Ahearns, ran their neighborhoods like "little republics."[35] However, the political exchange rate in machine politics was patronage or favors in exchange for electoral support. Given this exchange, the one thing citizens could not purchase with their vote was neighborhood democracy. The machine could not sell participation without eroding the centralized structure from which patronage and favors flowed.

On balance, the most that can be said of the old-time neighborhood bosses is that they established little baronies. And this is testimony to the existence of feudal power, not neighborhood democracy.

The reform reaction to the machine is too well known to warrant detailed description. The important point is that none of the progressive reforms increased neighborhood power. The main reforms, especially nonpartisan elections and at-large constituencies, stripped away whatever neighborhood power might have existed under the machine. The former militated against local political organization, and the latter was designed to vitiate "narrow" neighborhood-based interests and loyalties. The second major goal of reform was to place urban government in the hands of expert administrators, practicing techniques of scientific management, so as to separate administration from the venal business of politics. This goal was pursued through the establishment of city manager government and by the creation of even more independent boards and commissions. The practical effect was to fragment urban institutions, not to decentralize them. A strong argument can be made that the purpose, as well as the effect, of the reform strategy was to relocate the control of centralized power: to take power out of the hands of bosses and give it, still centralized, to upper-class reformers and their "neutral" experts. Indeed, this is the conclusion that recent scholars of the reform era have advanced, among them Samuel Hays, who argues that:

> While reformers maintained that their movement rested on a wave of popular demand . . . , they were in practice shaping the structure of municipal government so that political power would no longer be broadly distributed but would in fact be more centralized in the hands of a relatively small segment of the population.[36]

As other research makes clear, that segment was composed of a civic elite drawn from the chambers of commerce and other business-dominated community groups whose purpose was to "kick the bums out" of city hall and return power to the patricians, to those who have the "city's well-being most at heart."[37] However, men of this background obviously could not expect to gain and retain power if they were dependent on the very immigrant votes that elected the machine politicians. The reformers' only recourse was to "concentrate political power by sharply centralizing the processes of decisionmaking."[38]

At the same time that the reform movement was channeling power into the central government run by experts and "good government" advocates, another kind of centralization was taking place in many cities. Through the process of annexation, city governments came to control larger areas and to contain new "neighborhoods" which previously had been governed as independent towns. According to Milton Kotler, this process led to the "imperial city," and in his view "imperial control" was achieved "in most eastern cities by the last decade of the nineteenth century."[39]

Considering that the reform movement led to a new kind of centralization, it is perhaps surprising that several important Progressive theorists were strong advocates of neighborhood democracy. Mary Parker Follett, John Dewey, and Robert Park wished to create small-scale, face-to-face communities where citizens would play a direct role in the governance of their small areas. As Follett put it, "We begin with the neighborhood group and create the state ourselves."[40] Distressed by the "disappearance of neighborly feeling in the city," Dewey wished to recreate "immediate community"; to reconstruct the web of neighborhood ties and institutions.[41] Robert Park called for a "new parochialism," for "more attention and interest for the little world of the locality"; and asserted that neighborhood organization was the "type of organization which can be made the basis of all kinds of co-operative enterprise—the basis, in fact, on which the local community will again function."[42] Although it is not unusual that a reform movement should contain divergent views, it is significant that the concern with neighborhood democracy existed in social theory, not in political action designed to restructure urban government.

A similar pattern can be detected in the development of city planning. In this century, the main application of planning has been in the production of master plans by centralizing planning agencies. In 1962, "of the 126 cities of more than 100,000 population only two were without a master plan, completed or in preparation . . . "[43] Also, beginning with the creation of the New York Regional Plan Association in 1929, city planners moved toward metropolitan and regional planning.[44] Yet, at the same time that the planning practitioners were working to centralize the planning of the city, a number of important planning theorists were advocating a neighborhood approach to urban problems.

The decentralist strain in planning theory appears in Clarence Perry's neighborhood unit plan and in the writings of Paul Goodman and Lewis Mumford. Perry's plan for creating cohesive neighborhoods as the building blocks of urban planning first appeared in 1929. According to James Dahir, describing the origins and impacts of Perry's ideas:

> The builders of American cities have customarily erected housing with little regard to the grouping of people into neighborhoods for constructive social living. The neighborhood unit plan proposes a means of correcting this laissez-faire trend in city growth. Its substitutes for the gridiron pattern of city blocks, a design in which optimum size neighborhoods would emerge, and with its own shops, schools, and community facilities . . . In such groupings, the

plan's sponsors urge, people can find friendliness, relaxation, convenience, and safety, as well as opportunity for citizenship activities on a manageable scale.[45]

In 1947, Paul and Percival Goodman articulated a plainly utopian vision of a decentralized urban society. In *Communitas*, they offered plans for small-scale "living-and-working centers" and emphasized the principle that there should be "relatively small units with relative self-sufficiency, so that each community can enter into a larger whole with solidarity and independence of viewpoint."[46] In 1954, Lewis Mumford reaffirmed this decentralist tradition, asserting that "neighborhood unit organization seems the only practical answer to the giantism and inefficiency of the overcentralized metropolis."[47]

Whatever prominence these neighborhood advocates may have had in intellectual life, the decentralist vision had little immediate impact on urban government. Although Perry's neighborhood unit plan did lead to some experimentation with planned neighborhoods,[48] the main practitioners of the neighborhood approach in the early part of this century worked independently of city government in creating settlement houses and community centers. The settlement house movement, beginning with Jane Addams' Hull House in 1899, was an attempt by private citizens to supply services and the sense of community that were not produced by existing governmental arrangements.[49] The community center movement, which Robert Park participated in, aimed at establishing the same neighborhood solidarity in middle-class neighborhoods that Addams and others hoped to create in poor neighborhoods.[50]

In the period between 1900 and World War II, urban political theorists were mainly concerned with state-local relations—with the perennial problem of "home rule."[51] And with the New Deal, political attention moved even more dramatically from the little "republic" of the urban neighborhood to the reformist role of centralized, national institutions. In the 1930s, only Saul Alinsky,· with his Back of the Yards Experiment in neighborhood organizing stands out as a preserver of the tenuous neighborhood movement in American politics.[52]

By 1957 Lawrence Herson was speaking of the "lost world of municipal government,"[53] and the dominant topic of conversation among many urban political analysts was the need for metropolitan government. According to Robert Wood, writing in 1959, metropolitan government "is likely not only to be better managed in the professional sense but more democratically managed as well . . . "[54] The corollary of Wood's argument was that small-scale, neighborhood-based government is inherently undemocratic and illiberal. In his view, the little "republic" will provide the "neighborliness of the village," but individual dissenters will be subject to "intolerable disdain." Under these conditions, neighborhood government can only be "autocratic."

In the 1950s, decentralization was not a pressing issue. The political mood was to strengthen the urban executive by creating strong mayor charters; and the fact that some cities had neighborhood-based police and fire services, advisory school boards, or citizen planning boards was incidental. It is instructive too that in Sayre and Kaufman's massive study of New York City, written in the late 1950s, there is only one reference to "neighborhood"—in a statement about the social and economic diversity of neighborhoods in the city.[55]

Neighborhood Democracy and the "Urban Crisis"

In part, a new awareness of neighborhood politics and problems grew out of the discovery of the "urban crisis"—understood in physical terms. The urban renewal program, underway in the 1950s, sought to reclaim decayed neighborhoods through slum clearance and new construction. Later, the Ford Foundation initiated a "Gray Areas" program that addressed the social aspects of neighborhood problems through the provision of various social services. But neither program went far in the direction of decentralization and citizen participation. As Dahl points out, in New Haven, where urban renewal was carried further than in any other city, citizen participation was limited to membership in a blue-ribbon advisory board, the Citizens Action Commission.[56] More generally, a *Wisconsin Law Review* study found that the New Haven pattern was a typical one, noting that citywide advisory committees served "only a limited role in satisfying the basic need to involve people in government."[57] A further implication of this pattern is underscored by Harold Kaplan and Langley Keyes, who contend that the success of renewal depended on limiting citizen participation and "on keeping the inhabitants of the proposed clearance area in the dark as long as possible in order to minimize their certain opposition to a program that was committed to tearing down their homes and their neighborhoods."[58] In fact, the major contribution of urban renewal to the neighborhood movement seems to have been the creation of a vehement opposition among residents and some urban analysts. As J. Clarence Davies points out, after the effects of renewal became clear, neighborhood residents in new target areas began to mobilize as effective protest and veto groups.[59] And for urban analysts, like Jane Jacobs and Herbert Gans, urban renewal stimulated a strong defense of old neighborhoods.[60]

In large measure, Ford's Gray Areas program, like urban renewal, entailed a centralized intervention into the life of urban neighborhoods. Again New Haven provides an example in its Community Progress Inc., established under the Ford program as a loosely-related agency of city hall.[61] Although Paul Ylvisaker, the architect of Ford's program, believed strongly in the need to reestablish a sense of community in poor neighborhoods, demands for neighborhood government or community control were not in the air in 1962.

This same pattern of limited participation can be seen in a third federal attempt in the early 1960s to deal with declining urban neighborhoods. One goal of the federal government's Juvenile Delinquency Demonstration program, begun in 1962, was to encourage the "coming together" of neighborhood residents to discuss delinquency problems. But citizens were typically limited to an advisory role.[62]

At the local levels, various neighborhood-oriented programs and organizations began to appear around 1960. Like the federal programs, the local initiatives reflected a heightened awareness of physical deterioration in old neighborhoods. New York City began a Neighborhood Conservation program in 1959 designed to "halt and reverse housing deterioration . . . and ameliorate social problems affecting sound though troubled neighborhoods."[63] Pittsburgh had a similar initiative in its Allegheny Council to Improve Our Neighborhoods-Housing, Inc.[64] And in Chicago, the irrepressible Saul Alinsky was developing the Woodlawn Organization as a powerful instrument in resident-led neighborhood action.[65]

If the discovery of urban decay was one reason for concern with urban neighborhoods in the 1960s, the emergence of the civil rights movement was the second. The leaders of the drive for racial equality could hardly avoid emphasizing the conditions of black neighborhoods as a way of making the fundamental point about social inequality. But at first, ideas of decentralization and neighborhood power were not central to the civil rights movement. The goals were integration and equal rights; and most urban neighborhoods, being segregated and unequal, were considered part of the problem.

In 1965, these two background forces came together in the War on Poverty and especially in the Community Action program. Neighborhood decay was to be alleviated by the exercise of community power—which often meant "black power." By now, there is a small library of research and interpretation concerning the War on Poverty and the experience of community action. Many analysts have attempted to explain what went wrong with the experiment in community action and citizen participation. Daniel Patrick Moynihan concluded that the goal in community action of "maximum feasible participation" of neighborhood residents produced only "maximum feasible misunderstanding."[66] By contrast, critics concluded that community action never meant power for the poor or, in our terms, power to the neighborhoods. The important questions about community action in this context are: (1) to what extent did the program establish neighborhood-based institutions and (2) to what extent did the program bring about citizen participation?

On the first point, community action was directly controlled by city hall in many cities. The dominant pattern was to have a citywide board, not a neighborhood one, determine policy. Further, since the Community Action Agency was a centralized citywide institution, "neighborhood organization" was often an afterthought, understood to mean "self-help" or "brokerage"—"a process by which organizers find clients for agencies or help clients redress their grievances with agencies." In 1966, Congress passed the Quie Amendment, which required that at least one-third of the members of community action boards be representatives of the poor. In most cities, this formula increased neighborhood power. However, in the judgment of one participant-observer, Sanford Kravitz, neighborhood power still was not adequate to deal with the large, centralized bureaucracies.[67] Putting the matter more bluntly, Richard Cloward, an architect of community action, concluded that the winning of neighborhood representation on citywide boards was an "empty victory" since these boards were centralized and the system of representation insured the continued dominance of established political interests.[68]

Given these structural constraints, how much citizen participation was generated by the community action program? According to a Brandeis University study of "community representation in twenty cities," one-third of the community action agencies displayed a "pattern of target area participation which results in no significant impact on the decisions within the CAA or on other community service organizations."[69] In another third of the cities studied, neighborhood residents were found to have a strictly advisory role in decision-making. According to Ralph Kramer, who studied community action in five California communities, neighborhood demands for power and participation had the primary effect of generating prolonged controversy and power struggles.[70] As is now well known, the strongest evidence that community action did not lead to widespread participation is found in the experience of local elections, in which representatives were chosen for CAP boards and councils. In these elections, according to Sar Levitan, "voter participation ranged from a low of one percent to a high of less than 5 percent of those eligible."[71]

In light of this experience, it is ironic that the Model Cities program, launched in 1968, was designed to avoid the excesses of "citizen participation" that Washington and many city halls objected to in the War on Poverty. With Model Cities, city hall would have ultimate control of programs and expenditures, and the language of the enabling legislation clearly indicated the more restrained conception of neighborhood participation. Although community action was launched with the vague mandate of creating "maximum feasible participation," the Model Cities program was intended to develop "means of introducing the views of area residents in policymaking."[72] On the other hand, Model Cities comes closer to a neighborhood approach to urban problems inasmuch as the program was designed to focus resources on specific urban neighborhoods. The actual impact of the Model Cities programs is still unclear. Before the Nixon administration moved to tighten city hall control over neighborhood programs, there was some evidence that residents in some "model neighborhoods" had come to dominate policymaking boards and had achieved veto power over programs and expenditures.[73]

As has been noted above, the controversy over community control erupted in 1968 over New York City's experiment in school decentralization. However, in the schools as elsewhere, the idea of power to the neighborhoods had few precedents. Before 1968, a small number of urban school systems had created citizen advisory boards at the neighborhood level. In the late 1960s there were experiments with community schools designed to serve as community activity and service centers.[74]

As before in urban history, many of the most aggressive initiatives in neighborhood organization grew out of private organizations and ad hoc citizen groups which operated without any government sponsorship. Aside from the settlement houses and church-related programs, a myriad of self-help organizations arose in the 1960s. Various studies have charted the growth of tenants councils, block associations, neighborhood organizations and loosely structured protest groups.[75] In retrospect, it appears that it was these voluntary associations that made the late 1960s seem a time of intense neighborhood organization and of strident demands for "power to the neighborhoods."

In sum, the idea of "power to the neighborhoods" has shallow roots in American urban history. We have seen that the natural state of urban government is fragmentation; and that as a result the political movements expressed by the machine, Progressive reforms, and strong-mayor charters have all sought to combat fragmentation by centralizing urban political institutions. Only since 1965, with community action, the Model Cities program, and the New York school experiments have even half-hearted attempts been made to develop neighborhood institutions and neighborhood power.

3 Decentralization: An Analytical Framework

Decentralization has different and conflicting meanings. In the current debate it is used to describe both community control and policies designed to extend city hall's initiative and control. As James Fesler has written, "decentralization is an apparently simple term. Yet the appearance is deceiving and often leads to simplistic treatment that generalizes too broadly, starts from a doctrinaire position predetermining answers to concrete problems, or concentrates on a single phase of decentralization to the exclusion of others."[1]

To understand the meaning and implications of decentralization, five questions must be asked: (1) what is being decentralized; (2) what do different forms of decentralization mean for center-local power relations; (3) who gets power in decentralization; (4) what are the justifications for decentralizing urban government; and (5) how will decentralization affect different urban problems?

The first question raises the problem that there are many different elements of government that might be decentralized: for example, intelligence gathering, program administration, administrative accountability, and control of fiscal resources.

All political systems contain some elements of decentralization. It is my intention that the different elements can be ranked as follows in terms of the degree of decentralization that they entail:

1. Intelligence gathering—stationing officials in localities to find out what is going on in the field;
2. Consultation and advisory planning—seeking out the opinion of local people on policy matters;
3. Program administration—making local people the administrative agents of central government programs and policies;
4. Political accountability—establishing elected officials at the local level as representatives of local interests;
5. Administrative accountability—making district or neighborhood administrators responsible for government programs and accountable to local citizens;
6. Authoritative decisionmaking—giving localities control over policy and program development; and,
7. Political resources—giving localities control over fiscal resources such that local decisionmaking involves real stakes and capacities.

In short, the more decentralized the system, the more elements it contains.

If decentralization extends only to a program administration (elements 1-3), the system is still strictly hierarchical. If decentralization extends to "shared" decisionmaking and shared control over resources, the result is *shared power*. Finally, if decentralization extends to the point where the locality is dominant both with respect to decisionmaking and control over resources, the result is *community control*.

The Logic of Power Relations in Decentralized Systems

This analysis assumes that there is a logic of decentralization that explains the patterns described above. Consider a political system in which there are at least two levels of government and in which the center holds total power. Imagine further that the center is forced to devolve more and more functions to localities although at each stage it wishes to retain as much power as possible. What would the center do under these conditions?

The center would first decentralize functions that directly support it and that involve no direct transfer of power. Driven further, the center would create new forms of political and administrative authority so as to expend the number of power centers in the system. In this, the power trade-off would not be zero-sum. Rather than directly giving up its power, the center would manufacture new power and responsibility. Driven still further, the center would reach the point where power transfers become zero-sum, where any further devolution to the locality entails an equivalent reduction in central power.

Now apply this logic to the elements of decentralization. Central government is giving nothing away when it seeks to gain information about local conditions or canvass local opinion or administer programs at the local level. The second stage in the decentralization process is reached when local officials are elected to represent local interests and when local administrators are held accountable to local citizens. This stage represents a broadening of political and administrative accountability. It does not represent a direct redistribution of power from the center to the locality. For this reason decentralization as *community control* occurs only when control over decisionmaking and resources are devolved to the locality. Only at this point is the balance of power between center and locality affected, for now a zero-sum game exists in which the locality and the center are fighting for the same core of power.

Power to Whom? Political and Administrative Decentralization

Who receives what kind of power at the neighborhood level as a result of decentralization? In the current debate, three alternatives are raised. One alternative, "political decentralization," emphasizes citizen participation. The degree of participation varies in different plans and can change from the establishment of advisory boards to the creation of elected neighborhood councils. In political decentralization, neighborhood participants do not control local government administrators and employees.

A second alternative, "administrative or command decentralization," increases the power of existing neighborhood officials and administrators. The idea is to increase the flexibility, authority, and accountability of those public employees who deal directly with neighborhood problems. Administrative decentralization usually does not involve citizen participation.

The third alternative, "community control," gives neighborhood residents both political control—in policymaking—and administrative control of government employees. Thus, there are three different approaches to decentralization; and in each, power is given in different ways for different purposes.

Justifications of Decentralization

Why decentralize? Is decentralization an end in itself? Presumably not. Is it because centralized government has been judged a failure and decentralization is one alternative? Presumably, a more substantive justification exists. Decentralization must be a means of producing some desired end. But if so, what is the causal nexus that is presumed to exist between decentralization as a means and the ends it purports to serve. And further, what is the imagined impact on urban problems if those ends are achieved.

In discussions of decentralization, four justifications frequently arise based on psychological, administrative, economic, and political assumptions. The *psychological* justification is that decentralization will make citizens feel closer to government. As a result, government will become less remote and citizens less distrustful. The *administrative* justification is that decentralization will make government more responsive. The logic is that decentralized government, because it is more proximate, will have greater knowledge of local conditions and a greater capacity to react quickly to local demands. The *economic* justification, which bears some relationship to the administrative one, is that neighborhood government will become more efficient in resource allocation. The logic is that decentralized government can better identify community priorities both as between different services and within particular services and therefore allocate resources to the community more efficiently.

Finally, the *political* justification is that decentralized government will produce a strong indigenous political leadership, which will be better able to (a) mobilize the neighborhood for collective action and (b) articulate local interests in the larger community.

Having outlined the means-end logic of different justifications, the next step is to consider what the impact on urban problems will be according to the various justifications. A distinction is made between direct and indirect impacts. A direct impact exists if decentralization is a sufficient condition of the desired result. This is the case with administrative and economic justifications. In both cases, the desired end is entailed by the means to it. That is, government becomes more responsive by being more responsive. The only question is how great an impact greater responsiveness will actually have on urban problems. Similarly, greater efficiency in resource allocation is an end in itself.

By contrast, on the psychological justification, it is not enough that government be brought "closer to the people." It is necessary further that this proximity translate into a greater sense of trust and efficacy and that government perform in such a way as to justify a more positive attitude on the part of citizens. Similarly, with the political justification, it is not enough that indigenous leadership be created. It is necessary that the new leadership stimulate collective action in the community and articulate local interests more powerfully. In these cases, the impact is indirect since the desired result depends on contingent events after decentralization is established.

Further, what is the *range* of the impact produced by decentralization according to the various justifications? To answer this question, we need to distinguish different kinds of urban problems.

First, there are urban problems that cannot be solved without a substantial commitment of resources. In the category of resource problems are the shortage of adequate housing for low-income residents, the lack of recreational facilities, and the absence of hospital facilities or public transportation. The identifying characteristics of resource problems are: (1) they are bricks and mortar problems and (2) they require capital investment often on a large scale.

A second type of urban problem concerns government responsiveness; and it exists most prominently in urban public services such as fire, police, and sanitation. In these cases, the resident's complaint is often that the city did not respond—on time, or with concern, or with an understanding of particular needs.

A third urban problem can be called the *trust* problem and is manifest in education, police, and various social services. Here the complaint—voiced on both sides—is that parents do not trust teachers; residents do not trust police; welfare recipients do not trust case workers; and vice versa. The identifying characteristics of *trust* problems are (1) they involve constant personal interaction between citizens and public employees and (2) the service desired by both parties cannot be achieved without mutual cooperation and mutual agreement about goals and procedures. An example of this problem is that, as Albert Reiss has pointed out, the police cannot do their job if citizens do not report crime or support the work of the police.[2]

A fourth type of urban problem, rarely emphasized, concerns self-regulation. These problems could be remedied (or nearly so) if local citizens organized to control their own behavior (or that of family, friends, and relatives). The obvious problems of this type are smaller but still important: littering and dumping of garbage, malicious false alarms, arson, vandalism, and harassment of public employees. It is possible too that the development in the neighborhood of strong internal norms and regulations would affect drug problems and certain crime problems such as mugging and shoplifting.

Finally, certain problems require a restructuring of the relationship between urban government and other governmental units. Air pollution control is usually a problem of this type; and taxation, water supply, and gun control also fit into the category.

It should be clear that not every urban problem fits neatly into one problem category. Some, like law enforcement and education, are at once resource, trust, and responsiveness problems. If different urban problems have different characteristics, there can be no one solution to the urban problem. This means that decentralization is not an all-purpose remedy, but a policy that will affect different urban problems differently.

Correlating the different justifications of decentralization with the different problem types, we can see analytically how decentralization is likely to affect different problems. In Figure 3-1 we can see, for example, that if decentralization makes government more responsive, "responsiveness" problems will be

Justifications	Problem Types: Resource	Responsiveness	Trust	Self-Regulation	Restructuring
Psychological	–	?	+	+	–
Administrative	–	+	?	–	–
Economic	?	+	–	–	–
Political	?	?	+	+	+

Figure 3-1. The Impact of Decentralization on Urban Problems: Justifications and Problem Types.

affected, but not resource or restructuring problems. If decentralization makes resource allocation more efficient, resource problems will be affected, but not "trust" problems or problems of "self-regulation." Where the relationships in Figure 3-1 are uncertain, a question mark is recorded.

One implication of the analysis is that if the psychological and political assumptions are correct, decentralization is an uncertain policy instrument but one with the potential of affecting many urban problems. On the psychological justification, if citizens feel closer to government and increasingly powerful, they may demand more responsive service, have greater trust and confidence in government, and take initiatives in self-regulation. On the political assumption, if leaders mobilize their neighborhood and articulate neighborhood interests powerfully, this would have implications for most urban problems. (Mobilized neighborhoods might successfully demand greater resources and more responsive service and might be able to develop internal norms and self-regulation.)

Decentralization in Cities

At least nine different types of decentralization exist in American cities. They are: (1) self-help organizations; (2) advisory boards; (3) neighborhood field offices and little city halls; (4) ombudsman structures; (5) multiservice centers; (6) Model Cities programs; (7) community corporations; (8) neighborhood health corporations; and (9) community school boards.

1. Self-help organizations abound in American cities. They include block associations, tenants councils, neighborhood associations, and ad hoc protest groups. In some protest groups, the organizations have an advisory relationship with government and are not involved in what we think of as governmental functions. But many block associations, neighborhood associations, and tenants councils focus on service delivery.[3] They deal with garbage, housing, and crime problems. Some provide alternative services. In the extreme case, local citizens in Detroit, New York, and Chicago have formed community patrols to "police" the neighborhood. Other self-help groups have established day care centers and educational programs and have constructed vest-pocket parks. Regardless of their specific activities, all self-help organizations have several common characteristics. They are usually organized on a block-by-block basis, have democratic decisionmaking structures, and have no formal governmental power or authority. Such power and authority as they possess, de facto, is self-created and self-regulated.

2. Community advisory boards also abound in most American cities. A thousand citizen advisory boards were created during the War on Poverty alone.[4] In addition, advisory boards have been established in local school districts, mental health centers, police precincts, and in both urban renewal and Model Cities projects. New York City's community boards, which are authorized to

advise on all planning questions affecting their neighborhood, represent a relatively comprehensive and ambitious type of advisory board. In general, these boards are not democratically elected and lack any formal control over decisionmaking or resources.

3. Neighborhood field offices and little city halls have been established in many cities to "bring government closer to the people." They are street-level government offices that dispense information and sometimes administer programs. According to one 1971 study, twenty cities had little city halls (and five other cities had similar experiments with a different name).[5] Little city halls deal with a wide range of governmental functions from sanitation and recreation to welfare and employment. In some cases, as in Boston's little city halls, officials not only dispense information and process requests but also play an ombudsman role in pressing citizen complaints against city bureaucracies.[6]

4. Several cities have established neighborhood ombudsmen to represent citizen claims and complaints. Some of these ombudsmen work from central government offices; others work out of neighborhood offices. Some are city officials, others are community residents. The precise role of ombudsmen varies from city to city. It is clear that ombudsmen concern themselves with a wide range of government services. As to their power, one observer has noted that ombudsmen are often hamstrung by an "absence of subpoena power, inability to investigate *sua sponte*, poor records, lack of independence from the executive, and inadequate budgets."[7]

5. Multiservice centers delivering a wide range of urban services from a neighborhood location have been established in more than forty cities.[8] In these experiments, the degree of citizen participation ranges from membership on advisory boards to control of a board of directors that sets policy for the centers. In most cases, funding comes from the city government and is allocated to particular salaries and functions.

6. Model Cities programs were instituted in 150 cities. All have mechanisms for citizen participation although the extent of that participation varies from advisory planning to shared control. Programs are typically administered by a centralized city agency.[9]

7. There are 1,000 community corporations in American cities. Corporations differ from the Model Cities program in that they usually deal with a narrower range of programs and policies. Also, unlike Model Cities, citizen boards often administer programs under their authority.[10]

8. Neighborhood health centers differ from multiservice centers in two respects. First, they offer a narrower range of services; and second, neighborhood residents often control policymaking through an elected board of directors. Funding for these experiments typically comes in block grants from the federal government.[11]

9. The powers of community school boards vary widely from city to city, and it is therefore impossible to talk about a typical community school board. We

are concerned here with these elected neighborhood boards that possess a substantial amount of decisionmaking power and control over resources. New York City's community school boards are one example of this pattern, but in at least forty other cities, neighborhood residents have control of "at least one function in one or more elementary schools."[12]

Power Relations in Decentralization Experiments

Given the variations both within and between the nine types of decentralization, we cannot make precise generalizations about the status and range of decentralization experiments in American cities. Nevertheless, certain patterns emerge from existing experiments.

First, the ideal of community control has nowhere been achieved or approached. As Figure 3-2 makes clear, existing decentralization experiments either constitute the form of strict hierarchy or, at most, shared power.

Second, the degree of local power in different experiments varies inversely with the number of functions assigned to the local unit. The focused, single-function experiments possess more power than the more diffuse, general purpose experiments.

Third, relating local power to functional responsibility, we can see that existing experiments fall into three clusters. Leaving aside the case of self-help organizations which have no formal powers, there is a first cluster of three experiments where power is low and functional responsibility is wide. Advisory boards, little city halls, and ombudsman programs fall in this category. A second cluster, including multiservice centers, Model Cities, and community corporations, is characterized by moderate power and by a middle-range number of functional responsibilities. Finally, a third cluster, including neighborhood health centers and certain community school boards, is characterized by relatively strong local power and by narrow functional responsibilities. We can infer from these patterns that central government has given up its powers grudgingly. It has given up almost no power to any general purpose form of neighborhood government that might be viewed as a real alternative to central government. City hall has devolved substantial power only to experiments that either represent new facilities and resources (e.g., neighborhood health centers) or to strictly bounded experiments that have no possibility of challenging the general authority of central government (e.g., community school boards).

With regard to control of resources, no experiment comes close to full autonomy. As Figure 3-3 indicates, three experiments have virtually no resources at all; two receive grants that are tied to specific uses; three receive a combination of categorical and block grants; and only one, neighborhood health centers, receives the bulk of funds from block grants.

We have described three approaches to decentralization: political decentrali-

	Self-help Organizations	Advisory Boards	Field Offices & Little City Halls	Ombudsmen	Multiservice Centers	Model Cities	Community Corporations	Neighborhood Health Corps.	Community School Boards
1. Intelligence Gathering		+	+	+	+	+	+	+	+
2. Consultation and Advisory Planning	No Formal Powers	+	+	+	+	+	+	+	+
3. Program Administration			+	+	+	+	+	+	+
4. Political Accountability					Sometimes	+	+	+	+
5. Administrative Accountability			Sometimes	+	+	+	+	+	+
6. Authoritative Decisionmaking A. Some					+	+	+	+	+
B. Shared							+	+	+
C. Dominant									
7. Resources A. Some						+	+	+	+
B. Shared								+	+
C. Dominant									

Figure 3-2. A Scale of Decentralization in Neighborhood Experiments.

zation, administrative decentralization, and community control. What approaches have been taken in existing experiments? Most experiments emphasize political decentralization: citizen participation and some popular control of policymaking. However, a minority of experiments (little city halls, ombudsmen, and multiservice centers) emphasize administrative decentralization: devolving bureaucratic authority from "downtown" officials to neighborhood officials.

1	2	3	4	5
No Resources	Mainly Categorical Grants	Categorical Grants and Block Grants	Mainly Block Grants	Local Taxing Capacity
Self-help Organizations	Little City Halls	Model Cities	Health Corporations	None
Advisory Boards	Multiservice Centers	Community Corporations		
Ombudsmen		Community School Boards		

Figure 3-3. Control of Resources in Decentralization Experiments.

Finally, while no experiment comes close to controlling both policymaking and administration, some community school boards, health centers, and community corporations come closest to the ideal. In these experiments, neighborhood residents are involved in making policy, administering programs, and delivering services.

This study examines seven experiments that reflect the general pattern of decentralization in American cities. We examine block associations in New York as an example of self-help organizations; community boards in New York as an example of advisory boards; community task forces in New York as an example of ombudsman experiments; the Model Cities program in New Haven as an example of Model Cities; neighborhood corporations in New Haven as an example of community corporations; the Hill Health Corporation in New Haven as an example of neighborhood health centers; and community school boards in New York as an example of local school boards (albeit only those with substantial local power).

Part II
Experiments in Decentralization

4 Initiatives and Impacts

What impact do decentralization experiments have on neighborhood problems? To answer this question we must first see what initiatives are taken in various experiments. More precisely, how many iniitatives are taken (what is the crude "activity level")? How many initiatives are innovative (do not replicate existing programs and services)? How costly are the initiatives? Do initiatives have coherence (is there a strategy or an operative set of priorities)? Assuming that some initiatives are taken, we ask further:

1. Are initiatives tangible and visible?
2. Do initiatives develop over time?
3. Do initiatives produce measurable benefits?
4. Do initiatives *solve* any problems directly?
5. Do initiatives have second order effects—either positive ones such as the creation of new jobs or negative ones such as corruption?

The purpose of these "tests" is to provide explicit criteria for assessing the impact of decentralization. The logic of this approach is given in Figure 4-1.

Decentralization
Experiments Produce:

Initiatives	Impacts
Tests:	Tests:
1. Activity Level	1. Tangibility-Visibility
2. Innovation	2. Development over Time
3. Cost	3. Measurable Benefits
4. Coherence	4. Problem Solving
	5. Second Order Effects—positive or negative

Figure 4-1. Decentralization Experiments: Initiatives and Impacts.

Block Associations: The Limits of Self-help

Estimates of the number of block associations in New York range from two to five thousand. No one has made a systematic count. However, government records show that 500 block associations applied for small grants from an experimental program called Operation Better Block.[1]

The origins of block associations are unclear. Some residents trace existing organizations back to the block parties held before World War II for general enjoyment and after the war to welcome returning veterans. Some black residents in Brooklyn remember that block associations arose as property owners' organizations with the purpose of protecting newly purchased homes. By 1970, block associations existed throughout the city–in middle-class neighborhoods as well as poor ones. In particular, many block associations have sprung up in transitional neighborhoods–both those where young "brownstoners" are displacing low-income residents and those where signs of severe physical decay are unmistakable. Because of these historical patterns, block associations are often thought to be defensive and conservative: a device to avert blockbusters and low-income residents. There is some evidence for this view. Certain block associations grant membership only to homeowners, and others seem mainly concerned with keeping up appearances. The latter typically hang out signs admonishing neighbors to "keep your block clean"[2] and to remember that "your block is the front of your home." However, the majority of block associations include renters as well as homeowners, and many block associations have been formed in the poorest neighborhoods of the city where there are no property values to defend. What all block associations have in common is a strategy of self-help. They have turned to voluntary collective action to solve everyday problems of garbage collection, housing maintenance, and crime.

Applications to Operation Better Block reveal the dominant patterns of block association activity. In 1968, at the beginning of the program, the dominant concerns were beautification and "clean-up." Block association leaders wanted money to plant trees, install new street lights, and, most especially, to organize tenants to clean up garbage, vacant lots, and littered streets. The latter projects were typically organized for Saturday or Sunday mornings and were capped by block parties, using Better Block monies to purchase refreshments. The applications and expenditure audits show that most block associations began with block clean-ups, while tree planting and the purchase of street lights were more characteristic of middle-income blocks.

Many of the same block associations received money again in 1970, and the applications two years later indicate an expansion of block association activity. While the old concerns were still evident, many block associations were taking new initiatives: painting houses, making home repairs, renting storefronts for youth clubs or "senior citizens," working in traffic safety and developing "play streets" and vest-pocket parks in vacant lots. A minority of block associations took bolder initiatives: organizing tenants' councils and rent strikes; drug programs and crime patrols. Some associations established regular "complaint channels" with police and sanitation officials. Others organized to combat problems created by large private institutions such as hospitals and, in one case, the New Haven Railroad. One association in the South Bronx established a day care center; another in a middle-class neighborhood launched an extensive recycling project; and a third bought police whistles for residents on the block.

By 1971, many block associations showed high activity levels and a high rate of innovation. One Brooklyn newspaper, the *Home Reporter and Sunset News*, began a weekly column on block association events in Brooklyn, and an analysis of these columns from 1969-71 supports the impression of diversity and innovation.[3] The most active blocks reported a new initiative every few months. The search for innovations led to voter registration drives, housing rehabilitation, and block parties for neighborhood sanitation men (on the theory that if public employees know residents, they will do their job more carefully). Also, some block associations used their new organizing techniques to simply have fun: by painting flowers on lampposts, arranging ethnic folk dances, or taking bus trips to state parks.

Reports of block association presidents to Operation Better Block speak of concrete, visible accomplishments. Some presidents announced that they have "solved" certain problems such as littering, irregular garbage pickups, or drug peddling on the block. According to a report from one low-income block, "The children of the block swept three times a week which made quite a change for there was filth and broken bottles all over the streets."

A group in East Harlem reported, "We are in the process of getting the new storefront ready to have the following things: part-time nursery for working mothers, language classes, games for senior citizens, center for teenagers after school."

A block leader on the Lower East Side said, "After much discussion, it was concluded that there were many complaints and negligence on the part of the landlord and that some action was necessary. Calls were made daily to the Building Department as well as the landlords. After many days, the tenants were able to get some repairs done and a commitment from the landlord to finish all repairs within a certain period. There has been no complaints from the tenants since."

The most ambitious block associations have moved from one small success to another until they developed a wide-ranging neighborhood program. The Berkeley Place Association in Brooklyn began with "basic cleanup and tree planting" and then turned to health programs, youth programs, and "housing for the elderly . . . being displaced by rooming house conversions." The neighborhood Mothers Club of 148th Street in Harlem first established clean-ups and bus trips and then developed a summer youth program and a remedial reading program in conjunction with Teachers College. These associations, like others throughout the city, found that as they developed more ambitious programs it was necessary to both expand their neighborhood base (by involving nearby blocks) and to seek out relationships with government and private institutions.

Not all block associations achieved this pattern of cumulative development. More than 50 percent performed the simple tasks such as clean-ups but then failed to reach a new level of activity and subsequently declined. The two main developmental patterns may be represented as shown in Figure 4-2.

One reason for decline is that many of the simple problems do not stay

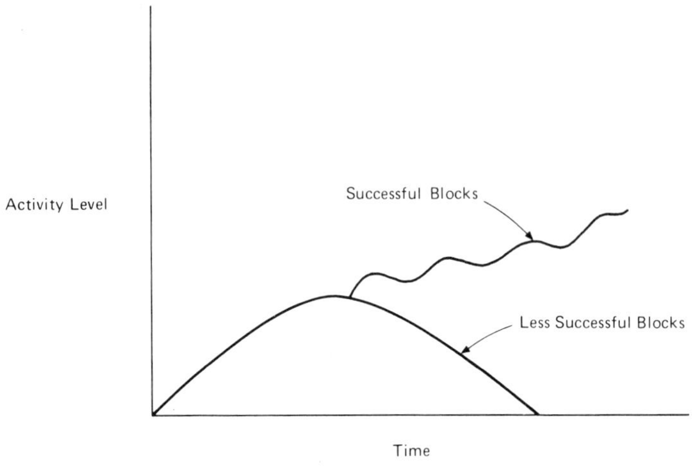

Figure 4-2. The Evolution of Block Associations.

solved. Garbage builds up again on the streets, and leaders report that neighborhood energies diminish with each new pickup. What was at first a novel act of neighborly cooperation becomes in time a chore. Also, having moved beyond the simpler problems, many associations find that their efforts produce diminishing marginal returns. And when problems such as drugs, crime, or education are approached, block associations find their organization has too narrow a focus. The problem becomes one of developing a neighborhoodwide constituency, but efforts to achieve such a constituency typically lead to time-consuming meetings and negotiations with other block and neighborhood groups. At this point, the flexibility and spontaneity that block leaders prize are lost.

Another reason for decline is that many block associations become heavily bureaucratic once the first stage of spontaneous action is over. Taking their role as "street-level governments" very seriously, some block associations develop elaborate committee structures and then have to devote considerable energy to keep the organization running. Committee work rather than focused collective action results, and at that point block associations become little different than the traditional "civic" coordinating committees that block leaders originally viewed with disdain.

Further, having met with early successes, many block leaders become seriously disillusioned when they encounter a problem in which proven techniques do not work. In the words of one Harlem mother, "We wait, wait, wait. Oh, they listen to your complaint and sometimes they even send somebody to fix it. But you wait first. And when it's not done right—and it never is—you can wait forever to have it corrected. So we just gave up."

Also, some problems simply cannot be solved by collective action, and this realization reduces the optimism that powers block associations. A Bronx block leader said, "I have watched the reaction to our efforts. It has become negative. We have several empty houses on the block . . . which are now fire hazards to the still occupied buildings. Some mothers tell their children to 'break down those houses'. What can we do. . . . The houses are now skeletons with glaring sockets of broken windows and doors."

Another dilemma of block association activity is that some "solutions" simply push problems onto the next block. This externality is particularly evident in block action against garbage dumping, drug addicts, and prostitutes. The result, block leaders admit, is that another block pays for the benefits that the organized block experiences.

In sum, in those relatively successful cases, block associations have a tangible and visible impact on daily problems. When successful, block associations produce what no government can: spontaneous collective action and self-regulation. As one block leader from the decayed East New York neighborhood put it, "There are times now when you see a kid speak to another about throwing garbage or pulling false alarms. That's something new."

Community Boards: Grievance Articulation and Sporadic Protest

New York's community boards are advisory bodies dealing primarily with physical planning and capital budgeting. Although informal boards existed in Manhattan as early as 1958, the boards, then known as community planning boards, were first given legal status in the 1961 City Charter. In this and in subsequent local legislation, the requirement has existed that the city consult the boards before making planning and development decisions concerning the neighborhoods. Today the boards still possess only advisory powers, and board members continue to be appointed by the borough presidents.

In practice, most boards play the role of a community forum in which local needs and grievances are articulated in a general way. In addition, many community boards attempt to serve as a clearing house for information on governmental programs and decisions; and some more ambitious ones attempt to devise plans for neighborhood development.

An examination of newspaper records and the minutes of six community boards indicates the dominant patterns of board activity. For one thing, the boards have a long and incoherent agenda. The agenda is, in effect, a catalogue of whatever problems have recently come to the board's attention and whatever claims and plans may happen to be voiced by board members or local residents. The tendency is for issues to remain on the agenda indefinitely and for relatively salient issues to be dealt with glancingly every few months for several years. The diffuseness of the boards' agenda is indicated by the following account: "CB #7 met for three hours and in those hours covered 23 topics. The litany of woes included nearly every problem–big and small–of life in a large metropolis of the nineteen seventies." Topics discussed included "dirty streets, urban renewal, crime, vest-pocket parks, noise, and nursing homes." Some topics were of special interest to various board members "who raised them briefly and then, usually referred the topics to the appropriate committee."[4]

The positive aspect of this procedure is that the boards do pay attention to the nuances of neighborhood life: the missing street sign, the defective traffic light, the broken park benches, the poorly maintained baseball diamond, and the storefront church threatened with eviction. But often discussion in community board meetings fluctuates between concern with particularities and concern with the most general problems of housing and education. Board minutes indicate that members consciously attempt to articulate broad community concerns so as to avoid factionalism and the necessity to choose between the priorities of different neighborhood groups. The result is a search for lowest common denominator issues and the articulation of "better schools, less crime" platitudes.

Another characteristic is that boards become lightning rods for community opposition to government initiatives. Since the role of the boards is reactive, it is not surprising that they operate as semi-institutionalized critics of government. Having developed this habit of criticism, community boards tend to adopt and amplify whatever antigovernment feeling is running in the neighborhood. The overwhelming majority of board resolutions are negative ones, and this has led some members to wonder if the board has become obstructionist–almost by reflex. One Queens board member said, "Even though most of our citizens are against this, aren't we obligated to think of the future and of the needs in 10 or 15 years? Are we always supposed to be against things?"[5] In the words of another member, "Community boards are still on trial. If they opposed every suggested improvement, then they would fail that test."[6] And further: "The easy thing to do is say 'stop–let's have no progress'."[7]

In general, the activity pattern of the boards is one of protracted debate and grievance-articulation punctuated by an occasional burst of protest. The normal complaint is: "We aren't getting anywhere." Or: "We went over this problem last month and last year and three years ago and five years." And when boards decide to protest city policies through demonstrations or meetings with officials or letters, the result is often frustration. Comments like the following appear regularly in board minutes: "Our powers are powerless." "It always seems to boil down to just sending a letter." But "the letters aren't answered and the calls aren't returned." The activity pattern of community boards can be expressed as shown in Figure 4-3.

Occasionally, protests bring results. Surveying newspaper accounts for the five year period 1966-71, we find that a board in Coney Island succeeded in

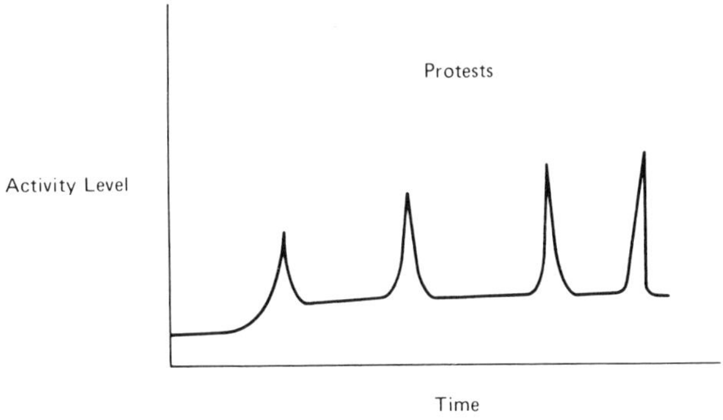

Figure 4-3. Activity Pattern of Community Boards.

saving homes from a planned industrial development and that a board in Queens was able to secure improved bus service for a local community college. Other boards persuaded the government to build vest-pocket parks and to stop high-rise developments. More substantially, community boards were active in the successful opposition to a plan that would have destroyed homes in Corona, Queens, and to the plans for a Lower Manhattan expressway. But with these more dramatic issues, the community boards were only one element in a unified community; and it was ad hoc groups that spearheaded the protest. At the same time, the evidence of board minutes is that frustration and defeat are the dominant pattern. Minutes of a community board in Manhattan show that an attempted challenge to policies of the Port Authority did not even provoke a reaction from the Authority. Community Board #3 on the Lower East Side enunciated five budget priorities in a 1969 meeting and discovered later that none of the budget requests had been approved by the Board of Estimate. Other boards in Manhattan fought against the construction of a large department store and a university library in their neighborhoods, but both store and library were ultimately built (although with some modifications). It is because of this experience that community board minutes are full of complaints that there is "no conversation" between city agencies and affected communities, or that "working with government is spinning your wheels in the sand." According to a Queens board member: "You can get more accomplished with a bunch of voluntary Kiwanians with a handshake and a smile than you can with all the meetings in the world with the whole city bureaucracy."[8]

A major reason for this frustration is that the boards themselves have difficulty making decisions, taking action and following through on their actions. On the first point, in an East Harlem board meeting, "no motions were made, no votes taken, no resolutions passed. . . . After more than two hours the meeting seemed to have accomplished a review of what the board already knew."[9]

On the second point, board meetings serve to elicit many ideas but not to mobilize political action. As one board member put it, "The question is who is going to bell the cat. It is a good idea to bell the cat, but who is going to catch him, hold him, and attach the bell. We need more than good ideas."[10]

The absence of follow-through is shown in the attempt of a Harlem board to develop a plan for community development. In 1969, the Harlem board undertook a neighborhood renewal study with the Columbia School of Architecture. A year later a 73-page report was completed that provided the basis for an extended "community planning conference" called "Harlem 1975." But in 1972, no action had been taken on the plan. The community board could not remember what happened to it, and city officials were hard pressed to find a copy in the files. The conclusion of one board member was simply: "We've seen it hasn't worked. The power structure hasn't given it a chance." The result in this and other instances is that community boards see no tangible, visible benefits resulting from their work.

The structural limitations of community boards are sharply depicted in the experience of the Lower East Side's Community Board #3 in the period 1963-71. Three patterns stand out. First, the board shifted its position between an inchoate agenda of new complaints and a number of long-standing issues that dragged on unresolved year after year. The effect of the former was to create a diffuse focus, while the old issues served to remind the board of the seeming intractability of government and of its own futility in achieving desired results.

Second, the experience of Board #3 shows that the costs of gaining information and access are very high for a group of citizen-volunteers holding full-time jobs and working only intermittently on neighborhood business. Board minutes are punctuated by reports of efforts to talk to city officials about neighborhood problems. "Mr. Kirchenberg plans to meet with Mr. Greenberg, operator of Avenue B bus line, to discuss improvements of service on existing roads."[11] In many cases, the board is unable to arrange a meeting with city officials for months. As a result, the subcommittees delay consideration and the issue is often never raised again. And if it is, it is with a sense of frustration that nothing has happened for six months or a year.

Further, lacking staff assistance, the board frequently defers issues until a detailed study is made or until a survey by one department or another is completed. The result is that the board is constantly waiting for information—information which takes considerable time for the board to develop itself or which is obtained from the government with difficulty if at all. One case that reveals the costs of information concerned the future of public markets in the neighborhood.

> The committee has been led to believe that the markets with the exception of First Avenue are not showing a profit. Mr. Lehman has stated that he is willing to accept suggestions and that he is making a survey scheduled for completion within several months. The committee is seeking complete information and definite statistics as a base for making recommendations.[12]

Finally, even when policy positions were arrived at, the board typically had trouble finding appropriate techniques of political action. As has been seen, the reflexive action is to write a letter "to memorialize the borough president," as various resolutions put it. The paucity of imagined techniques is clearly indicated in the board's discussion of ways to rally support for a low-income housing proposal. The advice of one member was to "organize a rally." "Rallies do not bring in votes and support," replied another member who wanted to ask local party structures to mobilize some support since "all major parties are represented on the board." Another member urged posting a "large sign," while another recommended that the board "purchase space in local papers and advertise the need for voters to support the proposition."

Even on critical issues, the board had difficulty determining a course of action. After several years of opposing the Lower Manhattan expressway with no result, several angry board members proposed that the entire board resign "provided that Local Planning Board #2 also agree to resign as a group." After lengthy discussion, the motion was put to a vote and defeated.

The Community Task Force: Neighborhood Ombudsmen

One complaint made by middle-income and low-income urban residents alike is that basic city services are going from bad to worse, and there is nothing the average citizen can do about it. And while the city's perceived failure to pick up gargage, remove snow, fill potholes, and repair catch basins may be viewed by the poor as further proof of city hall's indifference, for residents of working class and middle-income neighborhoods these service failures often create special bitterness and anger. One Queens housewife said: "Services are the only thing we get for our tax money anyhow, and, if we don't get them, what's the use. What's the use in trying to make a nice neighborhood if they don't pick up the garbage."

The Community Task Force in New York City is a response to this dissatisfaction. It operates in two middle-income neighborhoods: the Ridgewood-Glendale area of Queens and the Bay Ridge section of Brooklyn. While other areas of the city have Urban Task Force offices that handle citizen complaints, only these two areas have experiments in which citizen-volunteers assume the role of neighborhood ombudsmen. In Ridgewood and Bay Ridge, task force members receive service complaints from other citizens, report them to district superintendents, foremen, or police captains, and then perform "follow-up" surveillance to make sure that services have been delivered. What is innovative about this experiment is that neighborhood residents take responsibility for handling service complaints, and they have a direct and personal relationship with district officials. Task force members are assigned as "unit chairmen" for different services, and with the assistance of the mayor's office are introduced to the appropriate neighborhood official. Once a personal relationship is established, the unit chairman and the local official are often in daily contact, and together they assign priorities to different service requests and trace the city's response and remedies. Examining the records of the Ridgewood Task Force, we find the following typical service requests:

Complaint: Sunken manhole at intersection of Farmingville Ave. and 77th St. Bus hits the manhole and all homes shake; sidewalks are beginning to crack.[13]

Park at Central Ave. and 70th St. in very bad need of repair. Littered with glass and cans and one slide is missing and the other covered with tar. Bathroom facilities nonexistent.

Bulk pickup not made in area all week and resident has had couch out on street for two weeks.

Auto body shop on First Ave. is polluting the air with paint spray used on cars. They leave doors open while spraying, and both odor and flecks are all through the area.

The process that ensues when complaints are received is revealed in the following case concerning garbage pickups in Bay Ridge.

12/23/70. Caller says garbage not picked up for a week. Unit Chairman contacts sanitation counterpart.

12/26/70. Garbage picked up across the street but not on right side.

12/29/70. Garbage still not picked up. Sanitation foreman says garbage should have been picked up. Will check to see if route's not being followed.

1/4/71. Garbage picked up.

There was a substantial delay in getting service delivered in this case. In general, there is likely to be a delay in getting requested services delivered when the ombudsman has to pick his way through the city bureaucracy to find the right official and the right information. Thus, even when citizens deal directly with government, the costs in time and energy of gaining information and access often remain high. For example, when a complaint was received that "fluorescent lights were out under the elevated on Queens Boulevard," the Ridgewood Task Force set out on the following obstacle course:

This service request took some time for the following reasons: First called into traffic and they do not repair these lights. Then called Transit Authority and they referred us to Broadway Maintenance. This company installed lights but when called they said they did not repair same. Told us to call second company. This company said, after many conversations, that they would ordinarily repair these lights but had not received a contract from Traffic to do this particular job. Called Traffic explaining problem. They will give contract for repair of lights.

At its most effective, the Task Force is able to get services delivered within twenty-four or forty-eight hours. And in these cases, the impact is both tangible and visible for the affected individuals or block groups.

In general, the task forces have achieved substantial "activity levels." In a six month period, the Ridgewood Task Force reported that it had acted on "35 air and noise pollution problems, 195 pothole and other road repairs, 45 parks repairs and recreation requests, 190 sanitation problems, 80 traffic requests . . . and 100 water requests." By its own estimate, the task force was able to render "good, quick service delivery" in 85 percent of these cases, and an analysis of the daily logs kept by two unit chairmen suggests a clearance rate of at least 75 percent within forty-eight hours. The Ridgewood Task Force now receives an average of fifty service requests a week—the majority concerning garbage, potholes, and catchbasins. An analysis of Task Force records shows that the majority of these requests come from existing civic groups in the area; and, in this sense, the Task Force is right to say it exists to "serve civic associations" as well as individual residents. As to developmental patterns, it is significant that the Ridgewood Task Force seems to have reached an equilibrium at fifty requests, while activity in the Bay Ridge Task Force stabilized at a lower activity level and then began to decline. One explanation for this pattern is that the task forces have limited contacts in the neighborhood and therefore a limited constituency. Further, having achieved a tangible and visible impact on service problems, the task forces have mounted few new initiatives. This may simply reflect the negative side of the experiment's greatest accomplishment: the unit chairmen have learned how to play a focused role well and are sticking to that job.

Not surprisingly, the task force ombudsmen are most successful in handling relatively straightforward service delivery problems concerning potholes and catchbasins. Unit chairmen speak of having "mastered" the process by which service complaints are handled in these areas. The reasons for this success are clear. On the one hand the task force offers a simple channel of communication "to civic groups and residents" with service complaints and, further, has been able to visibly demonstrate the efficacy of the ombudsman technique. By contrast, before the task force, "civics and individuals had a tough time building businesslike working relationships with the district officials. . . . Each individual had to make his own contacts and then remake them each year. It seemed that the only way to get action was to press extra hard on the person we managed to get on the phone."

On the other hand, the task force experiment has eased citizen pressure on district officials in two important ways. First, district officials were accustomed to receiving a daily barrage of irate telephone calls—many repeating the same complaint. With the unit chairmen at work complaints are collated, and the source of the complaint is someone the official has worked with regularly. Second, district officials previously received many inaccurate or confused complaints, and the result was that trucks would be dispatched to the wrong street or with the wrong equipment. The task force mitigates this problem by checking both the nature and the location of the service problem.

The most common failure of the ombudsman technique comes with complaints in which there is either a need for capital expenditure or where higher level governmental decision and action are required. Thus, the task forces in Ridgewood and Bay Ridge had little success in remedying problems involving park maintenance and repair, traffic light installation, and air pollution control.

The future of the two ombudsman experiments is unclear. Task force members speak of the need to widen their constituencies and to move more vigorously on the "tougher" neighborhood problems, but, as with block associations, there would clearly be diminishing marginal returns in mounting these more ambitious initiatives. For the moment, task force leaders are sticking to what they know and do best.

Model Cities: Fragmentation and Political Conflict

The Model Cities program in New Haven began with an unusual amount of neighborhood control, but has evolved into a city-neighborhood partnership characterized by confused responsibility and authority. In 1968 the Hill Neighborhood Corporation (HNC) received an initial Model Cities planning grant. In 1969, the city agreed to give the Hill Neighborhood Corporation majority control of the City Demonstration Agency (CDA), the body responsible for directing the "action phase" of the program. The degree of neighborhood control provided by these arrangements was considered "bold, daring, unique, and far-reaching"[14] by the city's Board of Aldermen. But the federal government did not share this enthusiasm. In June 1970 the Department of Housing and Urban Development (HUD) decided that the neighborhood-controlled City Demonstration Agency "should become no more than an advisory board."[15] HUD ruled that neither the CDA nor the Hill Neighborhood Corporation "may operate the projects" and further that city hall must have ultimate power and authority over Model Cities. With this decision, neighborhood leaders became junior partners in the program they once controlled and a complicated administrative structure resulted. Under the new arrangements, the Model Cities program was administered by a new City Demonstration Agency whose director was appointed by the mayor. The old neighborhood-controlled CDA became the advisory City Demonstration Board. The Hill Neighborhood Corporation retained a role as the "citizen participation component" and was responsible for developing resident task forces in policy areas such as education, housing, and health. Since Model Cities was now a part of city government, the Board of Aldermen exercised legislative review over the program, and the Board of Finance fiscal review (see Figure 4-4).

The immediate result of administrative reorganization was to confuse the role of the Hill Neighborhood Corporation. Two years later HNC and the City Agency were still fighting over the definition of that role, and each blamed the

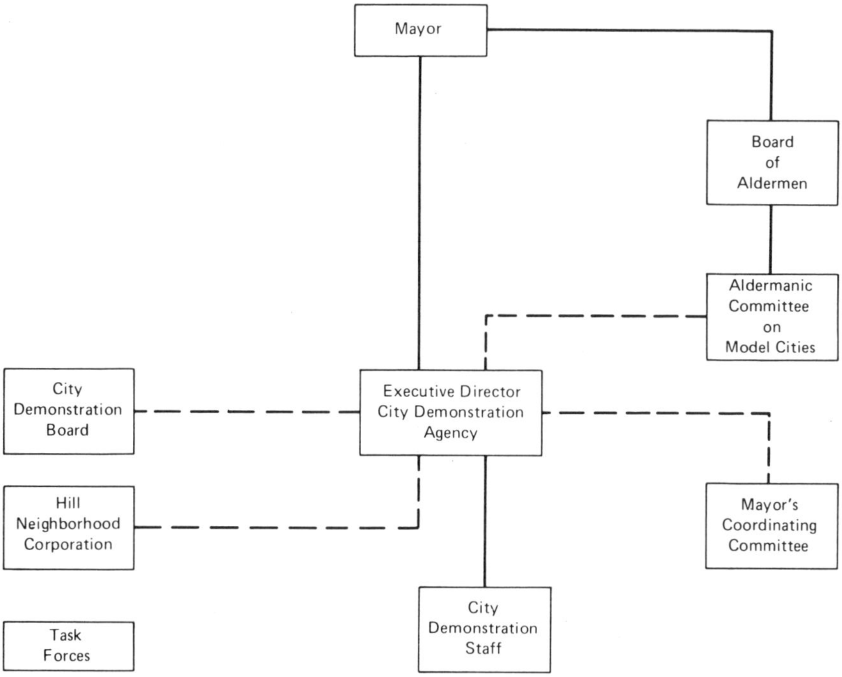

Figure 4-4. Structure of New Haven Model Cities Program.

other for the acknowledged failure of HNC to stimulate widespread citizen participation. In a 1971 report, the City Demonstration Agency claimed that the performance of HNC was "spotty," that cooperation between the organizations was "poor," and that "no evaluations were submitted on projects."[16] CDA's central charge was that "apparently the neighborhood corporation functions under the assumption that it is the administrative agency for the Model Cities program."[17] Further, according to the city, "there is a duplication of effort . . . and thus citizen participation and resident recruitment are neglected."[18] The Hill Corporation rebutted these charges bitterly. According to the neighborhood, "HNC has never seen the CDA contract to know for sure what functions CDA was legally bound to perform. . . . The CDA staff took a long time to hire and an even longer time to perform administration, coordination, and data collecting. As to planning, HNC Board and Task Forces have continued to feel that this role should be played by residents." As a result, HNC felt it must continue in its administrative role: "to carry the ball . . . fill in the functions which CDA was not carrying out."[19] The neighborhood supported its rebuttal with a list of services that the neighborhood performed without any help from the city.[20]

This continuing conflict has been focused on the annual budget allocation to HNC. The city regularly threatens to reduce funding unless the neighborhood does "what it is supposed to do." The neighborhood argues that cuts are designed to destroy citizen participation and increase the city's ability to use the program for political patronage. The source of this conflict lies in the fundamentally different interests of the city and the neighborhood, but the conflict is reinforced by the fragmentation of responsibility. Fragmentation also produced frustration among other partners in the program. Task force members complain that the city does not listen to their recommendations, and members of the City Demonstration Board complain that the Board of Aldermen ignore their recommendations. One member said, "What is the sense of making decisions night after night if the Board of Aldermen keeps going over our heads on everything we pass."[21]

Fragmentation is manifest in other ways too. First, since the Model Cities program seeks a comprehensive approach to neighborhood problems, the various policymaking bodies deal with the whole litany of urban troubles in the most general terms. Therefore, as with the community boards, the Model Cities agenda lacks coherence and a sense of priorities (beyond the platitudes that housing, employment, and education are critical problems).

Second, in moving from general concerns to specific programs, Model Cities adopts a piecemeal "add-on" strategy, allocating funds to government agencies and to various neighborhood organizations. This allocation pattern reflects the fact that Model Cities is an inclusive, coordinating device in which existing agencies and neighborhood groups play a prominent role. With all these interests involved in the allocation of resources, a fragmentation of effort is inevitable. As one neighborhood leader put it, "If you have one pie and twenty people are told they'll be fed, you're bound to get pretty small slices."

The fragmentation of funds also produces a fragmentation of day-to-day control. A number of Model Cities programs are operated by the Board of Education, others by the Police Department, Parks Department, Housing Authority, and the Public Library. When a new neighborhood program is begun, operating authority is often delegated from the city agency through the Hill Corporation to the community group. According to Model Cities reports, many such projects experience "start-up delays" due to the difficulty of mobilizing citizen participation. Thus, the administration of the Model Cities experiment is fragmented both horizontally (between Model Cities and other city agencies) and vertically (between Model Cities and various neighborhood organizations).

These patterns of fragmentation have two implications for the Model Cities experiment. First, because of the fragmentation of funds and projects, the costs of getting information about different parts of the program, much less of evaluating programs, are high. Minutes of the City Demonstration Board show that the board spends much of its time simply trying to find out what is going on in the program. For the same reasons, almost no systematic evaluation is performed in the experiment.

Second, because of the diversity of interests, political conflict results when the benefits to different interests do not meet expectations. Although piecemeal incrementalism is the logical policy for the city agency seeking to satisfy its many constituents, neighborhood groups feel that this policy creates a system of indiscriminate payoffs. The result is a constant barrage of accusations against the program by dissatisfied interests. As we have seen, the Hill Neighborhood Corporation believes it has been betrayed by the City Demonstration Agency. In 1969, Puerto Rican members of the corporation felt that their community was being "ignored," and five of the six Spanish board members resigned.[22] In 1971, a three-way shouting match over Model Cities policy and hiring practices developed between several aldermen, the chairman of the City Demonstration Board, and members of the Hill Corporation. So, too, city officials have charged that HNC has "broken down," and neighborhood organizations have argued that the city has deliberately ignored the desires of Hill residents. In 1971, another three-way conflict arose between the director of the City Agency, the director of the Neighborhood Corporation, and the chairman of the HNC board, with each accusing the other of undermining attempts to develop citizen participation.

Because city hall is involved in Model Cities, political conflict often leads to charges of "political interference." The city-appointed director is called a "dictator" and a "city hall pawn," and the chairman of the City Demonstration Board has been called a "lackey" by various neighborhood leaders. Charges of political interference are particularly salient in arguments about hiring. The CDA director reported in 1971 that Model Cities had created 200 new jobs.[23] Neighborhood groups argue that community residents should receive more jobs and accuse the mayor of using Model Cities as a tool. The accusations far exceed the available evidence on patronage hiring, but there have been several reported cases of local politicians and their friends receiving jobs "donwtown" in the City Demonstration Agency. Also, one leader in the Puerto Rican community resigned as a Model Cities official in 1971 citing "political pressures" to support the mayor and complaining that the program is "much too involved in politics."[24]

In this climate of fragmented authority and political conflict, Model Cities made few innovations and had little tangible impact on the neighborhood. Many programs simply added funds and personnel to the Board of Education or the Police Department; and others involved the funding of preexisting neighborhood organizations. Model Cities did create an imaginative sanitation project in which unemployed residents were hired to clean up the neighborhood. However, two other major innovations have collapsed. An experiment in economic development, Taking Care of Business, Inc., had a "minimal" impact. According to the CDA evaluation, "no businesses have received loans guaranteed through T.C.B." The agency's explanation for this failure is that there was a lack of "assistance," "clear direction," and cooperation between CDA neighborhood institutions. The second major innovation, the Hill Housing Development Corporation, has built no housing and will either be reorganized or disbanded.

The main impact of Model Cities has been in the creation of new jobs, especially in the two central administrative organizations, the City Demonstration Agency and the Hill Neighborhood Corporation. In an attempt to gain control of the program, the two staffs have been expanded to the point where administrative overhead costs account for more than a third of total Model Cities expenditures. Ironically, despite this emphasis on central administration, the political structure and programs of the Model Cities experiment remain deeply fragmented.

Neighborhood Corporations: Survival and Search for Effectiveness

Neighborhood corporations developed in New Haven as a way of decentralizing Community Progress Inc. (CPI), the city's antipoverty agency. They were the result of an evolution toward neighborhood-based policymaking and administration that began almost as soon as CPI was started. In 1963, a Neighborhood Services Division was established to stimulate "indigenous leadership in order that responsible citizens develop a concern for their neighborhood and an awareness of the problems and methods for solving these problems."[25] In 1965, a representative from each of CPI's seven target neighborhoods was added to the central policymaking board, and a twenty-one member Residents Advisory Committee was organized "to counsel CPI on the most pressing needs of the neighborhoods." By 1968, CPI had announced a commitment in principle to decentralization and the intention to take the "long jump from neighborhood representation at the policymaking level to actual operation of programs by [neighborhood] corporations."[26] From the time of this commitment, it took three years for neighborhood corporations to get legal status as delegate agencies of CPI. In the interim, neighborhood organizations were given a "dry run" administering summer antipoverty programs. During this period, the energies of both CPI officials and neighborhood leaders were directed at "the complicated and time-consuming mechanics" of decentralization.

However hesitant the process, the goal of decentralization articulated by CPI was bold: "self-determination and self-rule by the neighborhoods in community action."[27] More specific goals were also enunciated:

1. The encouragement of increased citizen participation.
2. The development of new vehicles of communication.
3. The promotion and development of innovative approaches for the solution of neighborhood problems.[28]

In 1972, eight neighborhood corporations were in operation—seven representing geographical neighborhoods and one, the Junta for Progressive Action, representing Spanish-speaking residents throughout the city. In most cases, the corporations were built on existing neighborhood organizations, such as the Dwight Concerned Citizens and the United Newhallville Organization. They were required to hold regular elections to provide neighborhoodwide representation.

The structure and functions of the neighborhood corporations vary in particulars but are similar in basic design. Each corporation has an unpaid board of directors and a paid staff of at least a director, assistant, secretary, and part-time bookkeeper. Each corporation has an office in the neighborhood, and some have more elaborate facilities—such as a teen lounge or community center. In addition, each corporation is given a limited amount of funds for year-round programs; and together, the corporations divide an allocation for summer programs (amounting to $160,000 in 1970). The Hill Neighborhood Corporation represents a special case since it is the citizen arm of the Model Cities program and therefore deals with a broader range of programs and policy decisions.

The most important difference between corporations concerns prior experience and stage of development. The corporations in Dixwell, Newhallville, and the Hill have functioned as neighborhood institutions since the mid-1960s. The corporation in Fairhaven, a racially mixed area, developed in the course of decentralization after 1968, and the Wooster Square Corporation, in a predominantly white, working-class area, is still being organized.

Despite these differences, several important patterns of initiative and impact appear in all the corporations. First, neighborhood corporations construe their mandate in exceedingly broad terms. Created to deal with "neighborhood problems," they have sought to attack the most general and intractable problems, such as education, housing, and employment. The West Rock Neighborhood Corporation set the goal of "achieving and maintaining good personal health for all citizens of West Rock."[29] The Wooster Square Corporation decided to attack the problem of "drugs, health, communication and community participation, housing, employment, and education." The Dwight Corporation enunciated goals of providing low-cost housing, a large enough health center to provide full family services to the residents of the Dwight area, and two day care centers within easy walking distance for "any resident of Dwight." The Fairhaven Corporation aimed to establish a "facility which can deliver comprehensive care in the areas of health and social services."

Many of the goals set by the corporations could not be achieved with the resources available. Also, the blueprints depended heavily on the support of government agencies, contradicting the basic premise that the Corporations can have an impact independently.

One corporation president wrote:

> We can begin the move by understanding that the establishment of a community services building which would house a number of agencies is but a beginning point. Beyond that point there will be an increasing need for those agencies involved to sit down and discuss and negotiate a common front. . . . In other

words, each agency will have to become critical of its own operation and enter with other agencies a process of evaluation whose only guideline will be the needs of the target area.[30]

Having outlined an ambitious five-year plan for solving neighborhood problems, the corporations typically developed an elaborate committee structure to formulate programs in the different problem areas. The Newhallville Corporation, for example, created seventeen committees—ranging from an education committee to a newsletter committee. The general effect of this proliferation was to reinforce the diffusiveness and incoherence created by the corporation's vague goals. The narrow effect of the committee structure led corporation members into extensive information gathering and long-range planning. The work of one Newhallville Committee was to:

Check all service agencies that service the community (V.N.H., welfare, Red Cross, etc.). What services do they have that we can utilize? Are they responding with assistance to Newhallville residents? We want to decentralize these agencies. Hopefully we will have them hire a Newhallville resident to fill a community position.[31]

Similarly, the Hill Corporation launched a survey of 1,600 residents in order to assess needs and complaints concerning education. The Dwight Corporation began its work on health problems with a lengthy study of health needs and available services.

This tendency toward information gathering and long-range planning is strengthened by two other characteristics of the neighborhood corporations. First, the corporations lacked the staff to design and administer specific programs, and they lacked the resources to initiate new programs. In this context, planning was often seen as the only available course of action.

More important, corporation leaders claim they never know from one month to another what resources they will have for the summer or for the next year. As a result, corporation directors and chairmen devote more time to funding problems than to any other part of their work. One corporation leader said, "We're always fighting for survival. It's like a game. We do it year after year, and we always get some money in the end. The way I see it, just surviving is a fulltime job."

At the same time that they are fighting to keep their experiments alive, corporation leaders recognize that they must "deliver" some tangible service or accomplishment if their support in the neighborhood is to continue. As one leader put it, "It's gotten so that people won't believe a word you say until you show them what you can do. It's that simple: Put up or shut up." Thus, the corporations must respond to two demanding constituencies: the higher level funding sources in government that want to see proposals and evaluations, and the street level groups that want to see concrete results. The problem of survival is double-edged.

In response to community pressures, some corporations have launched focused, innovative programs. The Fairhaven Corporation has developed a health clinic in an area where no health facilities existed previously. Several corporations have started day care centers, and others have opened teen lounges or senior citizen centers. Corporations that do not provide concrete services are searching for a way of "getting something going," as one leader put it. This search for effectiveness leads to ambitious proposals. The Fairhaven Corporation has received funds from a local foundation to start housing rehabilitation, and the Junta runs classes in the evening for Spanish residents who have a language problem in their jobs. Other corporations have been talking generally and with little result about starting factories to stimulate "economic development."

The demands of the two constituencies also force corporation leaders to spend much of their working day attending meetings around the city. On the one hand, there are numerous meetings "downtown" with CPI and other agencies whose activities affect the neighborhood. On the other hand, because a large proportion of corporation funds is delegated to smaller neighborhood groups, the corporation leaders must meet regularly with various delegate agencies to coordinate and review their projects. As a result, the activity levels of the corporations tend to be high, while the rate of innovation is relatively low.

Two other patterns exist. First, the open conflict that once existed between city agencies and neighborhood protest groups has been institutionalized through the corporations. Instead of protest and confrontation, protracted discussion and negotiation are characteristic of the relationship between city hall and the neighborhoods. Second, because of the uncertainty about funding and future programming, there is considerable shadowboxing between corporations and CPI. In general, this occurs when the corporations feel that CPI policy poses a threat to their independence and authority. In the first year of the experiment, the shadowboxing began when neighborhood leaders feared CPI support for the corporations was lukewarm. More recently, it arose over job control in summer programs.

Aside from the innovations mentioned above, the corporations' greatest successes have come through protest activity and ombudsmen-style case work. Corporation leaders believe that in recent years they have gained a substantial political education in the uses and limits of protest. As a result of their prior experience in neighborhood protest groups, they believe they know where and how to bring pressure, and recent events give some credence to this belief. The Dwight Corporation led a successful protest against a plan to tear down a building used as a neighborhood service center. The Newhallville Corporation was successful in its demands for a new school—and for citizen involvement in the planning of the schools—and has recently forced the city to reconsider a plan to run a bus line to the suburbs through their neighborhood. In these cases, the institutionalization of conflict between city hall and the neighborhoods has served to give the neighborhoods greater leverage and authority.

Because the neighborhood corporations operate out of visible storefront offices, they attract residents who have complaints about services, landlords, welfare administrators, or local school personnel. Indeed, several of the corporation directors assert that the channeling of complaints is the main service they perform—and the one with the most tangible benefits for neighborhood residents.

As against these "successes," the corporations' greatest failure is the inability to mount a coherent strategy and thus to avoid a total dependence on CPI programs and procedures. The corporations find themselves reacting to CPI decisions—"dancing for the piper," as one leader put it. This reactive posture is illustrated by the fact that the corporations spend almost half of every year trying to develop and operate a summer program to CPI's satisfaction. There are second order benefits in the summer program, for the corporations receive from twenty to fifty job "slots" that can be used to reward loyal supporters. But this "benefit" can become a liability to the corporations. In Wooster Square, for example, a majority of the corporations' low-income board members resigned from the board to get on the summer payroll.

At present, corporation leaders believe the future of their experiments to be highly uncertain. They fear that funding will be terminated; and, more importantly, that the experiments will not live up to their own high expectations. They feel that the corporations have had some impact, but worry that if they cannot solve "the big problems," residents will lose interest and so will the city government. In sum, neighborhood corporations constitute a promising, but unfulfilled innovation in urban government.

Hill Health Corporation: Building a Neighborhood Institution

The Hill Health Corporation is a neighborhood health center providing free health care to children of the Hill. The center was established in 1968 under a grant from the U.S. Children's Bureau administered by the Yale Medical School; and in four years, it has evolved into a neighborhood-run institution with a staff of 100 and a budget of over one million dollars.[32]

In 1968, at Yale's request, the Hill Health Council, a "community forum for health problems," established the Hill Health Board, composed of neighborhood residents and health agency representatives to oversee the workings of the health center. Under this system of participation, the personnel committee of the Hill Health Council hired all employees, and the Hill Health Board set policy for the "planning, developing, implementing, and operating" of programs in the center. In January 1971, the health center was incorporated as the Hill Health

Corporation, and a neighborhood-controlled board of directors replaced the Hill Health Council and the Hill Health Board as the governing body of the center.

After four years, several patterns of initiative and impact are apparent. First, the corporation clearly represents an important innovation: it supplies a service that did not exist before on the Hill. According to a 1968 survey, less than 50 percent of the families served by the corporation had "previous contact with the Visiting Nurse Association, private practitioners, or other sources of health care except the emergency rooms of the two local hospitals."[33]

The opening of the center provided Hill families with easily accessible health services adapted to their needs. Now, patients see the same doctors and nurses whenever they come to the clinic; they can request "home visits" by the nursing staff; and they have access to doctors twenty-four hours a day without having to wait in hospital emergency rooms.

Second, the corporation has expanded its patient registration steadily each year. Two thousand patients were enrolled in 1968; 4,000, in 1970; 6,000, in 1972. Visits by patients to the clinic averaged 400 a month in 1968, 800 a month in 1971. By 1972, the center averaged about 2,000 patient visits per month.

Third, the corporation has expanded services. In addition to services for children, maternal and family planning services were initiated in 1970; and adult health services in medicine, surgery, and dentistry were added in 1971.

This evidence demonstrates that the Hill Health Corporation is an innovative, responsive, and fast-developing experiment that serves all segments of the neighborhood. But it does not reveal the process of political and organizational development that made it possible for the center to become a viable neighborhood institution.

At first, the effectiveness of the Hill Health Board as a policymaking instrument was hindered by conflict between "militants" and "moderates." The former, who held the leadership positions on the board, took a strong position on hiring policy (they wanted only members of minority groups hired for staff positions) and on neighborhood autonomy (they wanted to force Yale and the Yale-selected director to give residents full control over the center's policies and programs). The moderate group wanted to get the experiment underway even if doing so meant hiring white doctors and waiting for community control. More important, the moderates objected to the "confrontationist" style of the board leaders and to the "rhetoric and verbal abuse" that filled board meetings. One participant said, "I got sick and tired of the shouting and the meetings that went on way after midnight and the fact that votes were never taken, and only a couple of people spoke. After a while, a lot of people stopped coming out. They couldn't put up with the language and the tactics."

This conflict involved incompatible personal styles as much as principle, and it was resolved when the "militants" became frustrated, and the leadership passed into the hands of those who "wanted to get on with it." Also, these neighborhood leaders faced a specific task. They were not protesting a highway or a renewal project but were trying to establish an intricate service facility. They were forced by the structure of their experiment to act on a concrete agenda; otherwise the leadership vacuum would be filled by the professional staff.

Another early problem concerned the role of agency representatives on the board. Because of their expertise and regular participation at meetings, agency representatives quickly became a dominant force—especially when, as often happened, only a handful of neighborhood people came to meetings. Moreover, before 1971, the board was in the awkward position of drawing all its members from outside organizations. Aside from the agency members, representatives were appointed by the Hill Neighborhood Corporation (HNC). Thus, the board did not claim the primary commitment of most of its members. Incorporation was designed, in part, as a response to this structural weakness. Nine "consumer" representatives (parents of enrolled patients) were added to the new board of directors. The idea was to mobilize the center's own special constituency as an instrument of self-government.

The board also confronted the power of the professional staff. Neighborhood residents were laymen trying to set policy in the technical field of health care, and it took time before organizational mechanisms were developed to give community people leverage in policymaking. Neighborhood control was established *de jure* by incorporation, but *de facto* control of the health center was achieved through the personnel and finance committees. The personnel committee existed from the start of the program and asserted its power in 1969 by accepting less than half of the professionals interviewed. Since then, through regular use of this power, the principle of neighborhood control of hiring has been clearly established. Every appointee is interviewed by the committee which attempts to "get a feel for the person . . . to find out if they are committed to what we're doing and if they're ready to stick with us after the thrill of *working with the poor* wears off."

Several other problems arose in the development of this neighborhood institution. Although the work of the board has generally been focused and coherent, the concern about the source and level of future funding has preoccupied and distracted board members. Like the neighborhood corporation directors, the Hill participants have never been able to elude the problem of institutional survival. The result is that much time is spent in developing and reviewing funding proposals and in lobbying for those proposals in Washington and in New Haven.

From the beginning, board members have also been preoccupied with the problem of mobilizing neighborhood support for the center. One member said:

We try to get the word out in the neighborhood newspaper (published by Model Cities). We think most people know about the center. But not enough people come to our meetings, and we worry that we might become just another service agency.

A related concern is that the center might lose its innovative spirit as it becomes more established. In 1969, the center launched an experimental lead poisoning program; but, in recent years, it has concentrated on maintaining and expanding its clinical services. One member said:

I know we're adding older people and new kinds of care and we're trying to get a health insurance program started. But I'm not sure we're getting out into the neighborhood enough. To make this a real community center, we should have a lot of outreach and a lot of good neighborhood workers.

Another member said:

Once you get a nice building and a good operation going, it's very easy to stay inside. We're all a lot more bureaucratic than we used to be.

In addition, the corporation has faced three other major problems. One difficulty which diminished when the corporation began to receive direct funding in 1971 was that both the Hill Neighborhood Corporation and Yale claimed some authority over the experiment. This led to occasional skirmishes between the university and the neighborhood and to a general sense that the center was "caught in the middle," as one board member put it. The initial project director, Dr. Alvin Novack, felt a conflict of loyalties that was exacerbated by the university's desire to deal privately with him on center policy. He solved this problem by refusing to meet with university officials unless neighborhood representatives were present. But even Novack, who was respected by Yale and the neighborhood people, could not always avoid being "whipsawed" by his two constituencies. One reason for his resignation was that Yale and the neighborhood representatives could not reach agreement on a job description detailing the powers and responsibilities of the project director. In general, Yale provided a convenient scapegoat for people with complaints about the center's policy. When the personnel committee made a controversial hiring decision, dissenters immediately charged that a "Yale conspiracy" lay behind the decision.[34]

Two other problems persisted after incorporation. From the outset, the professional staff's turnover rate has been high. According to one board member, the center has a "Peace Corps problem. People want to get the experience and they want to help poor people. But after a while they move on. What makes me mad is that other programs are so eager to hire our people away *after* we've given them the experience. Why can't they train their own damned people and stop raiding us."

Further, the larger the number of patients and the more extensive the services offered, the longer the waiting lines at the center become. Board members worry that, as one put it, "if the waiting lines get much longer, our center is not going to be much more responsive than the hospitals. We can't let that happen, but we need money and staff to keep it from happening."

Despite these problems and uncertainties, the Hill Health Corporation has achieved two important goals: the delivery of needed health services and the development of a viable neighborhood-run institution.

Community School Boards: The Costs of Participation and Ambiguous Power

New York's community school boards are the outgrowth of the controversial experiment in decentralization that began in Ocean Hill-Brownsville and two other New York neighborhoods in 1968. In 1969 state legislation established local boards in thirty-one city neighborhoods; and in 1970 elections were held to select nine-member boards. The boards have power, subject to collective bargaining agreements, "over the selection and assignment of personnel in the elementary, intermediate, and junior high schools within their boundaries."[35] The boards also have power "within the limits of contractual obligations entered into by the central board—over the allocation of virtually all funds spent on the schools in their jurisdiction."[36]

Originally envisioned as a radical approach to urban education, the decentralized boards established in 1969 constitute a modified form of community control.[37] Nevertheless the boards possess substantial power and constitute an important (and highly publicized) test of the hopes for decentralized government. Although it is too early to make definitive judgments about the success or failure of school decentralization, several patterns emerge from the experience to date that reflect basic structural characteristics of the experiment.

An analysis of board minutes in ten districts reveals that the local school boards are hard-pressed to keep up with routine housekeeping chores. According to the minutes, the dominant concerns in meetings are: (a) personnel matters—appointments, transfers, retirements, applications for vacation leave, (b) maintenance problems, and (c) allocation decisions relating to special federal funds (especially Title I appropriations under the Elementary and Secondary Education Act).

Thus, community boards are not primarily involved with lofty questions of educational policy but with the small details of school management. The reason for this is simple: the agenda of an experiment inevitably reflects the range of its mandate and responsibilities. The greater the range of service activities and the more complex the administrative structure, the more extensive the neighborhood agenda will be. Put another way, in a complex institution like schools, community participants face heavy overhead costs in merely achieving surveillance over basic school operations. One member said:

Almost every day the board is confronted with new issues and a realization that its own sources of information are severely limited. The result is steadily mounting pressure to devote more and more time to the district.

And further:

With 26,000 students, someone is going to have a problem every hour and come looking for us. The Board of Education can't handle its job, and I don't see any strong likelihood that we will be able to handle ours.[38]

Several other activity patterns appear. First, as was the case with neighborhood corporations, community school boards typically take a reactive posture: they respond to the problems generated by daily school business and by citizen requests. More precisely, the boards tend to react to and follow the proposals and initiatives of community school superintendents, principals, parents groups, and teachers.

Second, the burden of dealing with the complex school agenda makes it difficult for board members to develop a sense of priorities and strategy. One member in Brooklyn said, "Everything we do is piecemeal. We can't get away from the details—all those personnel items and all the routine business."

Third, like the community boards, the school boards have difficulty following through on decisions and initiatives when the agenda is always crowded with new issues. According to one PTA president in Queens:

Tonight as I reviewed briefs I've presented over the past 12 months, I was appalled over the fact that the questions raised are still the "questions of the hour," i.e., I could have chosen at random any brief, and it would have been relevant. It would appear that District 29 has stood still during the past 12 months; a rather sad fact to stand here and state.

In theory, the boards' greatest flexibility and discretion comes in the allocation of funds. In practice, the boards are locked into a pattern of incremental budgeting. For one thing, there is no simple "community interest." The debate at board meetings reveals that each school in the district retains its own priorities and interests and that there are conflicts over priorities both within individual schools and between different subneighborhoods. Also, before the boards came into existence, each school received annual allocations for special programs and put various programs into effect. As a result, when the new boards make allocation decisions, they face ongoing programs and strong expectations of continued support. Rather than completely disrupt these programs and antagonize established constituencies, the boards tend to make only marginal changes.

Second, lacking extensive staff resources for research and evaluation, the boards are unable to make confident judgments about the merits of existing programs. Consequently, they are dependent on the evidence and impressions presented by those who administer existing programs. At the same time, some boards have tried to mount ambitious evaluations, and these attempts have typically led to prolonged debate about the merits of different consultant firms and the role of evaluation.

More generally, the community school boards have become the apex of an elaborate pressure group system in the neighborhoods. Rather than becoming a self-centered forum for community participation, the boards exist alongside other mechanisms for participation and have, in fact, generated a new, more fragmented participatory structure. Preexisting parent associations and teacher groups continue to function; and, in many districts, advisory councils of parents and teachers have been established along with numerous student advisory groups.

Because the boards are the apex of the participatory system, they become the obvious target of grievances and dissent. Minutes of board meetings show that they are the new lightening rods for dissatisfaction with schools, and some of the board members have been surprised that they should be blamed for causing the very problems they were elected to remedy. One board member said, "It seems that in a few months we went from being part of the solution to part of the problem. It's hard to know how to deal with that . . . it sure doesn't make our job very easy or pleasant."

While the boards are highly active (activity levels show little fluctuation due to the constant press of the cumbersome agenda), the rate of innovation is low. Several boards in nonwhite neighborhoods have appointed nonwhite superintendents. Some of these boards have taken the further initiative of recruiting bilingual personnel—especially as guidance counselors. In terms of educational innovation, boards in nonwhite areas have developed courses in Black Studies of Hispano-American Studies; and at least two boards—on Manhattan's West Side and in the South Bronx—have created experimental learning centers for students with language and reading problems. And as with other decentralization experiments, the community school boards have provided a new mechanism for articulating interests and pressing specific grievances.[39]

Also, as was the case with neighborhood corporations, patterns of political behavior and action that were learned before decentralization are employed almost reflexively by school board members. Their problem, as they see it, is that their powers are ambiguous. Their response, as before, is often to blame local school problems on the policies of the central board. Faced with budget cuts and the need to lay off school personnel, the boards often attempt to mobilize the community in defiance of the central board. One effect of this response has been the creation of the same shadowboxing that sapped the energies of the neighborhood corporations in New Haven. A second effect has been to reinforce the sense of powerlessness that the boards were designed to combat. Community School Board #3 in Manhattan has devoted much of its time to mounting law suits against the central board. The result has been a test of important issues, but the strategy has led the board into another frustrating round of "assaults on the system" One member said:

When we started, we felt we weren't going to have to spend all our time trying to fight City Hall. We were going to be able to do things ourselves, harness our own resources. But we've been drawn into the old fight again and the story's always the same. You win some battles, but you lose the war and you wind up worn out and discouraged. The system always wins in a war of attrition.

Another member of this board concluded from this experience that there is little hope of solving problems in one urban neighborhood before fundamental changes are made in the larger political system.

Up to this point we have been attacking these problems in a piecemeal manner. We fire a principal here, initiate a lawsuit there, and try our best. Unfortunately, our best has not been good enough. Change has been slow and difficult. Also, the amount remaining to be changed is monumental. There is an urgent need for vast restructuring of the laws regulating the schools (not to mention areas like housing and health care).

There are two alternatives open to us. We can follow the course which we have been pursuing, or we can attempt to strike out in a new direction. The most effective way to change the laws, I think, is to change the people who write the laws.

The ambiguity of the boards' power is further revealed when members try to make new policy on issues clearly within their legal authority. Some of the boards wanted to evaluate the performance of teachers to find out "where we're strong and where we're weak," as one member put it. Another added, "If we have to lay off some teachers due to the budget cuts, it would be nice to know that we aren't losing our best people due to our own ignorance and an arbitrary process." But when Community Board #13 in Brooklyn tried to take the initiative on teacher evaluation, it discovered that it was "stirring up a hornets' nest." The board first acted on the evaluation problem on September 9, 1971, passing a resolution that "directed principals, in consultation with the superintendent, to rank all teachers in the school in accordance with relative teacher ability." The resolution was made because "we have tried to increase the effectiveness of teachers, but we have no way of knowing how effective teachers in the district are." The resolution was debated in a public meeting on September 22, and the opposition was out in force. One teacher said, "The child is not a machine and teaching is not to be compared with production as in a factory. . . . How can teachers be innovative when they are constantly threatened?"

A representative from the UFT observed that she was "disconcerted because we have at no time been consulted or made aware that such a move was in the offing. This is a very undemocratic way of getting the pulse of the pedagogic staff in the district. They are doing the best they know how to do, often under difficult circumstances." A principal commented that "this method of rating had once been considered by the state. After investigation, it was felt that it would be most detrimental to both teachers and children, in the area of human relations." After this discussion, the board voted to table the resolution. Nine months later, the issues was still tabled.

For all their efforts, the board members have not been able to produce tangible results. Although the board members interviewed believe that a spirit of innovation and openness has been established, they do not feel they have solved any important problems or even approached solutions. Reading scores in the city schools continue to decline;[40] violence and crime are increasing in schools in low-income neighborhoods; and attempts to deal with drugs, absenteeism, and the dropout problem have been unsuccessful.

Given the heavy demands placed on board members and the apparent intractability of school problems, it is not surprising that many board members have resigned their position. In the first year of the experiment, more than 10 percent of the elected members resigned.[41] These resignations were not random; they occurred most frequently in the poorest areas of the city. Some members resigned for personal reasons, but there is little doubt that the cost of participation in time, energy, and frustration was a crucial factor. One who resigned from a Brooklyn board said:

> I just found the amount of work impossible. I was attending meetings three or four nights a week, coming home at one in the morning. I couldn't do justice to my own job at the bank, and I wasn't much of a father to my two children. On top of that, I found that the board was always engaged in internal conflicts or tied down in procedural matters.[42]

The costs of participation are also felt by members who do not resign and are reflected in attendance problems at public meetings. Of the ten boards surveyed, four boards failed to reach a quorum of five members in half of the scheduled meetings over a one-year period.

When the citywide decentralization experiment began, some opponents, citing the experiment in Ocean Hill-Brownsville, predicted that the new boards would end up in stalemate if not chaos. Internal problems have arisen in many school districts, but in only five districts (out of thirty-one) have they reached crisis proportions, such that the board is barely able to function.[43] Significantly, the most critical problems have arisen in the city's poorest nonwhite neighborhoods. In East Harlem, a predominantly Puerto Rican neighborhood, newspapers have reported "deliberate disregard of rules and procedures."[44] Further, "community members and their children have been threatened. Public board meetings have been disrupted and coerced by special interest groups."[45]

In central Harlem, parent groups have charged that their board is a dictatorship and that they have been "intimidated, threatened, abused, and refused permission to participate in the discussions." On the Lower East Side, board meetings have been disrupted by fights between supporters of rival factions. In the district containing Ocean Hill-Brownsville, dissident groups have formally charged the board with "political favoritism and corruption." The minutes reveal that boards in other districts have experienced sharp conflict but were able to deal with it internally. However, many boards appear to do their work in a placid, businesslike fashion, and one, the Staten Island Board, is said to operate in "quiet isolation."[46]

Before and after decentralization fears were also expressed that teachers would be fired for political or racial reasons, that funds would be mismanaged, and that corruption and patronage would be rampant. Available evidence suggests that while these fears are not completely baseless, none of the problems are widespread.[47]

In sum, the community school boards have at least disproved a negative hypothesis: that decentralization will inevitably produce administrative chaos. But if this is a victory, it is a meager one—scored against the most pessimistic critics of the experiment. The fact remains that the community school boards have not been able to master the complex system they seek to govern, and they have not solved educational problems nor even produced tangible, visible impacts. Some neighborhood leaders feel that after two years they are finally making important changes. But they all agree that it will take the boards a long time to become effective instruments of neighborhood government.

A Comparative Assessment of Initiatives and Impacts

To summarize, we have examined the initiatives and impacts of seven different experiments in decentralization. Not surprisingly, we have found that the experience of decentralization differs dramatically from experiment to experiment. Some experiments have achieved impressive results: those block associations that stimulate collective action, the Community Task Force in getting quick action on service complaints, and the Hill Health Corporation in establishing a new delivery system for health services. Other experiments have had great difficulty in "getting off the ground." Their defenders would say they are experiencing severe "growing pains." Community boards have largely been unable to move from talk to effective political action; the Model Cities program has been crippled by internal fragmentation; and the community school boards have been frustrated by their ambiguous power and authority and by the task of mastering the Leviathan that is the urban school system. Finally, the neighborhood corporations have produced mixed results and are now struggling for survival from a position somewhere between "promise and performance."

Despite these differences, the experiments showed several common patterns on the nine tests of initiative and impact. The tests were: (1) activity level, (2) innovation, (3) cost, (4) coherence, (5) tangibility-visibility, (6) development over time, (7) problems solved, (8) measurable benefits, and (9) second order effects. The common themes were as follows:

1. In all experiments, some citizens have gained a forum for articulating their interests and grievances. In this sense, decentralization clearly produces a greater awareness of neighborhood needs.
2. All the experiments, except for community boards, are highly active and have introduced some innovations.
3. No decentralization experiment has produced quick and dramatic solutions to major neighborhood problems. While it is too early to judge the long-term effects of decentralization, decentralization appears to be most "responsive" to local needs when it produces concrete services that did not exist before—as with the Community Task Force and the Hill Health Corporation.
4. The experiments had the least success in showing development over time, "solving" problems, and producing measurable benefits. But these patterns reflect the intractibility of many neighborhood problems as much as the limited impact of decentralization.
5. More than half of decentralization experiments had significant second order effects on employment. And in two experiments, Model Cities and the community school boards, the fight over jobs was a dominant feature of the decentralization experience.
6. The experiments revealed that decentralization can be undertaken in several forms without great cost to the taxpayers. Of the seven experiments studied, only two—the Hill Health Corporation and Model Cities—required large expenditures as a necessary condition of innovation.
7. With the exception of block associations, decentralization experiments had little effect in stimulating self-regulation and collective action by "rank and file" neighborhood residents.
8. The experiments did not bear out the worst fears of decentralization critics. Charges of corruption and patronage-dispensing have been made against the community school boards and, to a lesser extent, Model Cities, but the experience to date does not confirm fears of administrative chaos and abuse of power.

On balance, the differences between experiments are more revealing than the shared patterns. In Table 4-1 the experiments are scored on the tests of initiative and impact.[48] The scoring system of high, medium (some), and low gives a

Table 4-1
Initiatives and Impacts: An Assessment

	Block Associations	Community Boards	Community Task Force	Model Cities	Neighborhood Corporations	Hill Health Corporations	Community School Boards
Initiatives:							
Activity Level	High 3	Low 1	Medium 2	Medium 2	High 3	High 3	High 3
Innovation	High 3	Low 1	Some 2	Low 1	Some 2	High 3	Some 2
Cost	Low	Low 1	Low	High	Medium	High	Medium
Coherence	Mixed 2	Low 1	High 3	Low 1	Low 1	High 3	Low 1
Impacts:							
Tangibility-Visibility	High 3	Low 1	High 3	Some 2	Some 2	High 3	Some 2
Development Over Time	Mixed 2	Low 1	Medium 2	Low 1	Low 1	High 3	Low 1
Problems Solved	Some 2	Low 1	High 3	Low 1	Some 2	Some 2	Low 1
Measurable Benefits	Some 2	Low 1	High 3	Low 1	Low 1	High 3	Low 1
Second Order Effects:							
A. Employment	Low	Low	Low	High	Medium	Medium	High
B. Corruption	Low	Low	Low	?	Low	Low	Some
	17	8	18	9	12	20	11

rough approximation of the patterns described above and provides a common denominator for comparing the various experiments. Assigning numerical values (high-3, medium-2, low-1) and tabulating the results, we find that the seven experiments fall into three groupings (see Table 4-2). Two experiments, Model Cities and community boards, receive low scores on almost all of the tests of initiative and impact. Two other experiments, neighborhood corporations and community school boards, are rated slightly higher—their impact is not negligible, but it is not substantial on the tests of tangibility-visibility, development over time, problems solved, and measurable benefits. Finally, the Hill Health Corporation, the Community Task Force, and block associations score high on almost every test.

These findings suggest two important conclusions about the impact of decentralization experiments. First, experiments dealing with concrete service problems seem to have a greater impact than experiments dealing with broadly-defined urban problems. The service-oriented experiments are able to achieve focused, coherent initiatives and produce visible results in the short run.

Second, the amount of impact achieved in the experiments is not related to the amount of power vested in the experiment. Decentralization advocates sometimes argue that the more neighborhood control, the greater the impact on neighborhood problems will be. Our findings do not support that belief. As Table 4-3 indicates, the variance between the "power" rankings and the impact rankings for the seven experiments is substantial. (The "power" rankings reflect the scale of decentralization presented in Chapter 3.)

Table 4-2
Summary Impact Rankings

1. Hill Health Corporation	20
2. Community Task Force	18
3. Block Associations	17
4. Neighborhood Corporations	12
5. Community School Boards	11
6. Model Cities	9
7. Community Boards	8

Table 4-3
Power and Impact in Decentralization Experiments

Experiment	Power	Impact
Community School Boards	1	5
Hill Health Corporation	2	1
Neighborhood Corporations	3	4
Model Cities	4	6
Community Task Force	5	2
Community Boards	6	7
Block Associations	7	2

5 Representation and Internal Democracy

Decentralization experiments seek to promote neighborhood democracy. But do they achieve that goal? In what follows, we put the seven experiments presented in Chapter 4 to the following tests of democratic structure and process:

1. Are the neighborhood leaders representative of the communities they serve? First, do they reflect the racial, ethnic, and economic characteristics of the neighborhood (social representation)? Second, since advocates often claim decentralization will open local government to previously unrepresented groups, do the experiments represent "new" interests as well as established community organizations? More precisely, does decentralization extend the scope of representation beyond that provided by existing participatory mechanisms?
2. Are leaders selected in democratic elections? If so, what form do the elections take?
3. What is the voting turnout in neighborhood elections? Does voter participation in the experiments exceed the minimal participation in War on Poverty elections?
4. How actively do neighborhood leaders participate in the work of their experiments? Are there high "dropout" rates and levels of absenteeism?
5. What is the pattern of leadership in decentralization experiments? Is it "one-man rule" or is leadership dispersed?
6. Are neighborhood leaders accessible and accountable to nonleaders?
7. How actively do nonleaders participate in meetings and in the work of the experiments?
8. Is there opposition to the leadership of the experiments? If so, how is this opposition expressed?
9. Do leaders follow democratic procedures in making decisions? Are meetings open? Are decision rules established and adhered to?

These tests focus on three criteria of democracy: (1) representation—whose voice is heard?; (2) polyarchy—leadership accountability and the control of leaders by nonleaders; and (3) internal democracy—adherence to democratic procedures and decision rules.

Social Representation

The seven experiments have a mixed record of social representation. Block association leaders generally reflected the racial composition of their block: they were white on white blocks and nonwhite on black and Puerto Rican blocks. However, on racially mixed blocks, the leaders were drawn from the older racial or ethnic group. On several white and Puerto Rican blocks in Brooklyn, the leadership was white; on several black and Puerto Rican blocks in the South Bronx, the leadership was black.

In economic terms, the block leaders were relatively successful members of their small communities. Most of them were white-collar workers, professionals, or the wives of white-collar workers and professionals. Several others were government employees and small businessmen. Block leaders also tended to hold jobs outside the neighborhood that put them in touch with the larger world of business and government. Many said that their outside experience with business organizations or government gave them the know how to get things done back on the block.

The members of community boards, in general, and Community Board #3, in particular, were relatively unrepresentative of their neighborhoods. In racially mixed neighborhoods, the newest racial groups tended to be weakly represented on the boards. In the Lower East Side's Community Board #3, until very recently, there were only two or three Puerto Rican members in a neighborhood that was over one-third Puerto Rican. From the outset, the white, largely Jewish population held an overwhelming majority on the board. In recent years, however, the borough president appointed more minority group members to reduce the racial imbalance on the board. Nevertheless, the white community still held a clear majority (although white residents were only a third of the population). As to economic background and occupation, previous studies have shown that professionals and local political leaders dominate the boards.[2] An analysis of Central Harlem's Board #10 showed the board to be an assembly of established neighborhood leaders in politics, business, the church, and major community organizations. The white membership of Community Board #3 was dominated by lawyers, party leaders, and local businessmen. The black, Puerto Rican, and Chinese members were, in almost every case, government leaders of major community organizations. In general, the community boards were dominated by what Merton calls "local notables."[3]

The two community task forces were located in white neighborhoods, and the task force members were almost all white males, born and raised in the neighborhood. As in the block associations, the task force leaders had a relatively high economic and occupational status. While the neighborhood residents were predominantly blue-collar workers, policemen, and firemen, the task force leaders were small businessmen, real estate brokers, and local professionals.

The pattern of social representation in Model Cities was mixed. Only three nonwhite residents who were not also political office holders participated on the twenty-one member City Demonstration Board, and they were leaders of community organizations. By contrast, the community task forces were run by ordinary neighborhood people—housewives, welfare mothers, and blue-collar workers. The pattern of social representation in the Hill Neighborhood Corporation was mixed. Although the black community was heavily represented on the board, the Spanish community and white residents of the City Point area were hardly represented at all. The black members, who constituted a majority of the board, included leaders of community organizations as well as welfare mothers, but four of the five officers were white residents—a minister, a Catholic nun, a small contractor, and a leader of a civic group.

Social representation was relatively strong in the neighborhood corporations. In the black neighborhoods of Dixwell, Dwight, and Newhallville, the leadership was overwhelmingly black and included blue-collar workers and welfare recipients, as well as ministers, community leaders, and local politicians. Again, social representation was weaker in racially mixed neighborhoods. In predominantly white Wooster Square, blacks and Puerto Ricans were not represented on the corporation's board. In Fairhaven, where large numbers of Puerto Ricans, blacks, and elderly whites live, the Puerto Rican and elderly white communities had little representation in the corporation. Because it has been difficult to organize these divided neighborhoods, board members tended to be new recruits to neighborhood politics rather than the leaders of established organizations. These new recruits also had more diverse occupational backgrounds than leaders in more organized neighborhoods. The Fairhaven Corporation, for example, included factory workers, teachers, housewives, union organizers and office workers.

The Hill Health Corporation exhibited relatively strong social representation. Blacks and Puerto Ricans dominated the board, as they do the population of the neighborhood. The only group that was not represented were the white residents who live on the periphery of the Hill. The board members also had diverse backgrounds; there were factory workers, office workers, and small businessmen, as well as the more traditional participants, ministers and employees in community organizations.

The community school boards provided weak social representation. Of the 279 board members elected in thirty-one districts in 1969, 72 percent were white while only 16.8 percent were black and 10.8 percent were Puerto Rican.[4] In six districts with a population of black and Puerto Rican pupils ranging from 30 to 48 percent, only five of fifty-four board members were nonwhite. In twelve districts where black and Puerto Rican pupils made up over 85 percent of the school population, only six had a majority of nonwhite members on the board. Further, more than half of the minority group members (forty-four out of eighty-seven) were elected from just six districts. These were the city's poorest, most segregated neighborhoods: Harlem, Spanish Harlem, the South Bronx, Bedford-Stuyvesant, and Brownsville. Thus, only forty-three minority group members were elected in the remaining twenty-five districts, and in ten of these districts, no minority group members were elected to the board. By contrast, the Central Harlem #5 was the only school board in the city without white representation. As to occupational background, board members were drawn disproportionately from professional, managerial, and technical positions (63.8 percent). For the rest, 10.3 percent were employed as paraprofessionals or by poverty agencies (mainly the minority group members), 5.3 percent were clergymen, 16.6 percent housewives, and 4.0 percent laborers, mechanics, "or other quasi-skilled or unskilled low-paying jobs."

Representation of New Interests

New interests were represented in few decentralization experiments. Those where "new interests" had achieved some power were block associations, the Community Task Force, neighborhood corporations in previously unorganized areas, and the Hill Health Corporation. Of these, the representation of new interests was strongest in the block associations and the task force. The block associations usually were a recent innovation operating closer to the grassroots than other community organizations. They also represented a first step in neighborhood organization that could be pursued at low overhead costs. They were an accessible instrument for neighborhood residents with energy and initiative. The Community Task Force also attracted new participants because it was a new experiment that was substantially different from other community organizations. Because task force members worked quietly "behind the scenes" with government officials, the experiment was not likely to attract those community leaders used to working in a visible, public forum. Thus, in both experiments, the main participants were citizens who were not leaders of entrenched community organizations and who made the experiment their main community activity.

The neighborhood corporations in Wooster Square and Fairhaven recruited new participants because, as one corporation member put it, this is "a new game in our part of town and anybody can play." However, because these corporations sought to be neighborhoodwide coordinating mechanisms, the leaders of powerful community groups were also recruited to give the corporations the desired breadth of representation.

New participants appeared in the Hill Health Corporation for two reasons. First, as with the other experiments embodying substantial "new interests," the health center was a recent initiative in a policy area that existing community organizations had not emphasized. The prominent community leaders on the Hill were chiefly concerned with urban renewal, Model Cities planning, and education. As a result, health planning was handled by a loosely structured Health Council. Second, the Health Corporation created its own constituency when it decided to elect board members from among its consumers. The consumer representatives were, by definition, ordinary citizens distinguished only by the health needs of their children. Along with some block association leaders, the consumer representatives constituted the newest interests—were the least experienced and established "leaders" in any decentralization experiment. At the same time, because it began under the auspices of the Hill Neighborhood Corporation, established leaders also played an important part in the Health Corporation. The two board presidents in the corporation's history were both prominent community leaders with experience in the Hill Neighborhood Corporation and in other community organizations.

In short, the experiments that represented "new interests" tended to be recent innovations and to be concerned with tangible problems of service delivery. Unlike the other experiments, they were not designed as formal deliberative bodies or structured as all-neighborhood assemblies. The other experiments were just that, and as a result, they had the participants appropriate to a federation: leaders representing established political and community interests. As we have seen, local notables dominated the community boards. Community Board #3, for example, included a city commissioner, two district leaders, five other city officials, and the head of the local chamber of commerce. Most of the Puerto Rican representatives were leaders of community organizations funded by the city or the federal government.

In New Haven Model Cities, half of the Hill Neighborhood Corporation members were representatives of major neighborhood organizations. The City Demonstration Board was dominated by aldermen and other political officials: a state senator, state representative, and city treasurer. Other members included the president of the Board of Education, the director of Junta (the Puerto Rican neighborhood corporation) and the wife of the director of the Hill Neighborhood Corporation.

Board members of the neighborhood corporations in the older black communities constitute what one member called "the long-time activists, the pillars of the community." In Dixwell, for example, the director was a former alderman, and the board was dominated by aldermen, ward chairmen, and officials of neighborhood organizations and agencies.

The community school boards, more than any other experiment, drew their members from well-organized interests. But, in that case, the interests were not merely established community organizations and party structures. Because school decentralization had obvious implications for educational policy, the teachers union (UFT) and the Catholic Church fielded candidate slates throughout the city. So did Parents Associations and Parent Teacher Associations in many districts. Of the 1,051 candidates who ran in the school board elections, more than 65 percent ran on slates. An analysis by the Queens College Institute of Community Studies of 279 successful candidates in twenty-five districts showed that the church and the UFT elected a majority of the new board members (95 and 46 members, respectively.).[5]

A survey of candidates for the local boards by the Public Education Association also reveals the background of candidates who were not affiliated with the organized slates.[6] According to the survey these candidates also did not represent new interests. They were long-time neighborhood residents who had held numerous leadership positions in community organizations. They were people who "enjoyed high preelection exposure and reputation."[7] The following sketches illustrate the sources of this exposure and reputation:

Candidate A: Past P.T.A. president and United Parent Association delegate, two years each. Executive Board member Educational Council, United Near Morrisania Educational Council, Screening Panel for Local School Board District #9.

Candidate B: Community Development Coordinator—Chairman, Community Board of Directors, E.N.Y.—Brownville Comprehensive Family Planning Program; Board of Directors, Planned Parenthood N.Y.C.; Board of Directors, Christians and Jews United for Social Action; Representative Member E.N.Y. Charrette Steering Committee; member, Parent's Association, Thomas Jefferson H.S. 1966-1968.

Candidate C: Homemaker. A resident thirty years in Woodside. Mother of 4. Education, Public School finished High School. Active Community Affairs. Member of 108 precinct Youth & Community Council. Elected 2 terms treasurer Youth Council. Worked PAL Play Street Program, Cub Scout Pack #221, President ISW Civic Association. Member PS 199 Parent Association.

In sum, the evidence on representation of new interests indicates that the more formal and comprehensive the mechanism for neighborhood government the more leadership will be recruited from established community and political interests. On the one hand, this means that leadership will be experienced and will provide a link between existing centers of power in the neighborhood. On the other hand, the effect of institutionalizing existing leadership patterns is to inhibit the development of new political leaders.

Democratic Selection

Leaders were selected in the decentralization experiments in three ways: by appointment, election, and a combination of the two methods. The borough president appointed all community board members. The mayor's office selected the first Community Task Force members, and then residents worked with the city to appoint the remaining members. Many block association leaders were self-appointed when they organized their blocks. Clearly, democratic selection was weakest in these cases.

In three of the experiments, roughly half the board members were appointed and half elected. The experiments with a mixed selection process were Model Cities, neighborhood corporations, and the Hill Health Corporation. In each case, the appointed members represented major organizations and agencies in the neighborhood.[8] Thus, only the community school boards and some block associations relied exclusively on elections in selecting neighborhood leaders.

Of the five experiments that elected some or all of their leaders, only the community school boards had "formal" elections characterized by nominations, petitions, campaigning, and secret ballot voting. There was no direct campaigning in the Hill Health Corporation elections. In block associations, Model Cities, and neighborhood corporations officers were elected in open meetings in the informal manner of church and social organizations. Formal nominating petitions were not required, and a nominating committee of current officers usually offered a slate of nominations that could be challenged from the floor. No campaigning took place, and voting was informal if the electorate was a group of friends and neighbors—as it was likely to be in the block associations and neighborhood corporations.

Voting Turnout

During the War on Poverty, voting turnout in neighborhood elections was minimal. Rarely did more than 5 percent of eligible voters participate.[9] Advocates of neighborhood control have argued that citizen participation would increase in time as neighborhood institutions became more established and citizens gained experience in neighborhood government. The decentralization experiments provided a test of that hopeful hypothesis. For if neighborhood residents gained a political education during the War on Poverty, this education should be reflected in greater citizen participation in the decentralization experiments of the 1970s. However, the record of the five experiments that held elections did not support the hypothesis. Differences in voting turnout can be explained by variations in the structure and scale of the experiments, but in general voting turnout was low. It was minimal in the formal neighborhoodwide assemblies: Model Cities, neighborhood corporations, and the community school boards. Only in the two service-oriented, smaller scale experiments, block associations and the Hill Health Corporation, did voter turnout far exceed 5 percent. In recent years, Model Cities elections never involved more than 500 voters, and frequently only 50 or 100 residents participated. The voting turnout in neighborhood corporation elections outside the Hill was no higher and, indeed, was usually lower. In Dixwell, for example, which has a well-established corporation, only 160 residents participated in a 1972 election. The same patterns existed in the Dwight, Wooster Square, Fairhaven, and Newhallville neighborhoods.

Voter turnout in the 1970 school board elections was marginally higher than in the latter experiments but was still nowhere near the voting turnout in citywide elections. The highest turnout in any district was 22.0 percent; the average was 13 percent; and less than 10 percent voted in eleven districts. Significantly, the average turnout in seven of the poorest, nonwhite districts in the city was 6.6 percent.[10]

By contrast, election turnout was far greater in the Hill Health Corporation and in some block associations. Five hundred consumers voted in the first Health Corporation elections at a time when roughly 1,000 families were enrolled in the program. This 50 percent voter turnout was surpassed in those block associations where single-family homes, two-family homes, and small apartment houses predominated. In these cases, which constituted more than half of our sample, voting participation often exceeded 75 percent; and in five cases, virtually every family participated in block elections. On those blocks where large apartments predominated which contained as many as 400 families, voting turnout was rarely above 20 percent.

Accessibility and Accountability

The more informal and small scale the decentralization experiment, the more accessible its leaders were to neighborhood residents. Many block association leaders were proud of the fact that "their door is always open" to neighborhood residents with problems. In their small area, block leaders can play the role of a "friendly neighborhood mayor," as one leader described it, naturally and unself-consciously.

The members of the Community Task Force were also easily accessible to neighborhood residents. In Ridgewood, the names and telephone numbers of the unit chairmen appeared regularly in the neighborhood paper, and flyers were distributed telling residents how to get in touch with task force members. Some task force members "made the rounds" of local church and civic groups to advertise their work.

Many leaders of the Hill Health Corporation regularly spent time at the Health Center to be available to neighborhood residents, and their names, addresses, and telephone numbers were listed at the center. Similarly, the most active leaders of Model Cities and the neighborhood corporations could often be found at their respective neighborhood offices. But the less active members tended to avoid this visible, public role. As these members saw it, their job was to go to meetings and make decisions, and they often said they did not have the time or the desire to "sit on the telephone all day talking about people's gripes."

Only in the community boards and the community school boards, both neighborhoodwide representative assemblies, were leaders not easily accessible to residents. Because these participants dealt with so many controversial community issues and had so many constituents, many board members felt they had to limit their accessibility. Many of these board members had unlisted telephone numbers and could only be contacted through their organizations.

Holding public meetings and publishing minutes and reports are other ways of making leaders accountable to nonleaders. In every experiment except the Community Task Force, public meetings were held at least once a month. The task force did not hold public meetings because the members believed that the ombudsman's function was best performed privately and quietly, with citizens dealing directly with individual unit chairmen.

The practice of reporting debates and decisions, through published minutes and announcements, existed only in the more formal neighborhood assemblies. Block associations, the Community Task Force, and neighborhood corporations operated informally, and did not produce a written record of their work. By contrast, Model Cities and the Hill Health Corporation kept detailed minutes and made regular reports, although the minutes of meetings were not available to neighborhood residents. Again, the community boards and the community school boards were the extreme cases. Having produced the least accessibility, they provided the greatest amount of accountability through published minutes and reports. In both cases, the records of meetings and decisions were available to neighborhood residents, and the community school boards, in particular, produced copious reports on their activities. The limitation of this form of accountability was that although each experiment published a financial statement (if it had a budget), none of the experiments opened its books to public scrutiny. In fact, much of the controversy in the community school boards and Model Cities concerned salary levels and alleged patronage appointments, and critics complained that they could not get the facts on these issues because they could not "see the books."

In sum, accessibility and accountability varied inversely in the decentralization experiments. The more informal and small scale the experiment, the greater the accessibility and the less the formal accountability. Conversely, the more formal and comprehensive the experiment, (e.g., community boards, Model Cities, and the community school boards) the less accessibility and the greater the accountability.

Participation of Leaders

When an alderman, congressman, or mayor is elected, the public normally expects that he will serve out his term and work actively for his constituents. But when a neighborhood resident is appointed or elected in a decentralization experiment, no guarantee exists of continued and active participation. In fact, the participation of leaders was high in small-scale experiments, and it decreased as the experiments became more comprehensive in their mandate and constituency and more formal in their democratic structure. Thus, the leadership of block associations and the Community Task Force remained constant over time and, according to first-person reports, leaders attended meetings faithfully. Neighborhood corporations and the Hill Health Corporation were also characterized by a continuing active leadership, although typically a sizable minority (as much as a third of the board) never attended meetings or participated in the work of the neighborhood corporations. In the case of the Hill Health Corporation, two-thirds of the elected consumer representatives quickly became inactive for reasons that will be examined below (see Chapter 7).

Turnover and nonparticipation increased dramatically in the three most comprehensive neighborhood institutions: community boards, Model Cities, and the community school boards. In Model Cities, the membership of the HNC board changed almost completely from 1968 to 1970, and again between 1970 and 1972. In addition, the turnout at board meetings was rarely greater than 50 percent, and vacancies were filled constantly because of resignation and nonparticipation. Leadership participation on the community boards was similarly casual and irregular. An analysis of Community Board #3's minutes for the period 1963-1971 shows an average attendance below 50 percent and attendance below 25 percent in a quarter of all meetings. Because of this widespread nonparticipation, community boards have been forced to set attendance rules as a way of eliminating "deadwood." As we have seen, the community school boards had a resignation rate of over 10 percent in the first year, and a majority of the ten boards studied had a recurrent problem reaching a quorum in public meetings.

Leadership Democracy and Power Sharing

To what extent is one-man rule the leadership pattern in decentralization experiments? To what extent is leadership shared by many participants? In this aspect of neighborhood democracy, the small-scale, informal experiments were less democratic. They tended to be run by one or two dominant leaders. This was particularly true of block associations which typically were started by one energetic block resident who became the president of the association and was, in many cases "a one-man show." According to a block leader in Brooklyn, "Frankly, without me, this whole thing would collapse. I put it together and keep it going and people depend on me for everything. When you come right down to it, I am the block association. I'm not sure the others would keep it going if I wasn't here to carry the ball."

In the Community Task Force, the chairman was the most active participant and dominant force. And in all neighborhood corporations, dominant leadership was provided by the paid director and the president of the corporation board. The Hill Health Corporation was guided from its inception by three prominent leaders, and two of these have held dominant control since then, serving successively as president of the corporation.

Only in Model Cities, the community boards, and the community school boards did many participants share leadership power. In Model Cities, neighborhood leadership was shared by the officers of the Hill Neighborhood Corporation, the City Demonstration Board, and the chairmen of the existing task forces. With the community boards, the officers and the chairmen of numerous policy committees formed a collective leadership. On the nine-man community school boards, there was little distinction in leadership power among active members. Each member was given primary responsibility for certain policy areas, committees, and schools in the district.

Participation of Nonleaders

With the exception of the block associations, widespread participation of nonleaders existed only in the formal neighborhoodwide assemblies—and especially in the community school boards. "Ordinary" citizens did not participate in the work of the Community Task Force and the Hill Health Corporation. In Model Cities and neighborhood corporations, large numbers of residents attended meetings in times of crisis, and then they were crucial to the mobilization of protest in the neighborhood. Similarly, residents became involved in community board activities when decisions affected their interests. Given the range of issues before the board, lobbying by one neighborhood group or another was a constant feature of board meetings. In the community school boards, participation of nonleaders took several forms. First, there was a variety of lower-level representative bodies such as parents associations, advisory councils, and local teachers' groups that articulated the interests of particular schools and constituencies. Second, neighborhood groups constantly lobbied the board or protested board policies. Third, large numbers of parents and residents attended board meetings to press a complaint, a request, or an opinion.

The same pattern exists for organized opposition within decentralization experiments. Only in the community boards and the community school boards did one find factional caucuses, bloc voting, and angry debate. The other experiments were characterized by a personalized, town meeting atmosphere in which consistent cleavages and opposition did not appear.

Democratic Procedures

A final test of internal democracy is adherence to democratic rules and procedures. In a formal governmental institution like a city council, we take for granted that an agenda will be printed before meetings, that rules of order will be used in regulating discussion, and that votes will be taken, recorded, and decided according to majority rule. In neighborhood institutions, however, because of deliberate informality in some cases and unregulated conflict in others, these procedures were not always observed. As before, block associations present a mixed pattern. Some held informal meetings in which no attempt was made to impose parliamentary procedures. In other associations, especially those in white working-class areas, procedures were taken very seriously. In some cases, one of the leaders served as official parliamentarian. Since Community Task Force members rarely made collective decisions in their meetings, the issue of democratic procedure did not arise. In Model Cities and the neighborhood corporations, the informal town meeting atmosphere was prized, and the emphasis was on consensus and tacit agreement. At the same time, minutes of the City Demonstration Board and first-person reports on the neighborhood corporations suggest that the town meeting ideal collapsed under the weight of conflict and controversy. Then the spirit of informality resulted in shouting matches. As one neighborhood corporation member put it, "We don't deal very well with conflict. On the hot issues, everyone talks at once, no motions are made; no votes are taken or if they are, they are forgotten or taken over if someone doesn't like the result." Because it makes authoritative decisions on concrete expenditure and hiring issues, the Hill Health Corporation is forced to adhere to democratic procedures. In corporation meetings, motions were made, votes were taken and recorded, and an agenda was published before every meeting. The community boards and the community school boards also attempted to follow formal democratic rules, but protest and disruption by community groups often made it impossible to do so. The minutes of community boards show that disruptions and informal filibusters were widely used by angry dissenters. In the case of Community Board #3, nonwhite members who constitute the minority faction acknowledge that they deliberately turned meetings into shouting matches to avoid having votes taken in which the white majority would triumph. A second tactic employed by the nonwhite faction was to "pack the meetings" with neighborhood people who "harrass the other side and prevent them from taking votes." Packing and disrupting meetings were other tactics used by dissident factions at community school board meetings. More generally, some of the troubled boards in low-income areas were rarely able to get through a meeting without disruption, and the tactic of confrontation was used widely in other districts as an ordinary lobbying device. According to one member of Community School Board #3 (on the West Side of Manhattan), "It is very easy for our opponents to shut us down. We often have 500 people at our meetings, and it doesn't take more than 50 protestors to make a shambles of the whole thing."

Thus it was in those experiments where opposition was well organized that the obstacles to democratic procedure were greatest. It is perhaps obvious but nevertheless important that the "virtues" of opposition and democratic procedure exist in delicate equilibrium.

Conclusion

How democratic are the experiments in decentralization? The summary assessment given in Table 5-1 and 5-2 indicates that one of the experiments came close to the ideal of neighborhood democracy expressed in the eleven "tests." (These figures are based on the same scoring procedures used in Chapter 4.) Only three experiments—block associations, the Hill Health Corporation, and the community school boards—received high marks on as many as five tests. Every experiment ranked low on at least three tests, and four experiments ranked low on five tests. On the other hand, the fact that all the experiments "passed" at least 50 percent of the tests indicates that decentralization yields some substantive gains in neighborhood democracy.

The summary assessment reveals other important patterns:

1. The evidence does not confirm the hypothesis that the greater the decentralization the greater the representation and internal democracy. Total scores differ little between the experiments and clearly do not rise with increased local power (measured according to our scale).
2. Each experiment had almost as many weaknesses as strengths in democratic process.
3. Most experiments failed to represent new interests strongly; most did not contain organized oppositions; most showed weak adherence to democratic procedures; and the majority continued to have low turnouts in neighborhood elections. No experiment gave representation to young residents—especially teenagers.
4. The most important variation existed between small-scale, service-oriented experiments and the neighborhoodwide representative assemblies. Let us take block associations, the Community Task Force, and the Hill Health Corporation as examples of the former; community boards and community school boards as examples of the latter. The small-scale, service-oriented experiments were strong in the representation of new interests and voting turnout, while the neighborhood assemblies were weak. They were strong in accessibility and weak in accountability, while the reverse was true of neighborhood assemblies. The small, focused experiments had strong leadership participation and were relatively weak in leadership democracy, participation of nonleaders, and organized opposition. Again, exactly the opposite pattern existed in the formal, neighborhood assemblies. Although these comparisons and contrasts do not apply in every case, they are firm enough to pose a significant puzzle. Why do these two types of experiments have opposite traits? Why is it that as

Table 5-1
Representation and Internal Democracy: A Comparative Assessment

	Block Associations	Community Boards	Community Task Force	Model Cities	Neighborhood Corporations	Hill Health Corporations	Community School Boards
1. Social Representation	Medium 2	Low 1	Medium 2	Mixed 2	Mixed 2	High 3	Low 1
2. Representation of New Interests	High 3	Low 1	High 3	Low 1	Mixed 2	Medium 2	Low 1
3. Democratic Selection	Mixed 2	Low 1	Low 1	Mixed 2	Mixed 2	Mixed 2	Low 1
4. Voting Turnout	Mixed 2			Low 1	Low 1	High 3	Low 1
5. Accessibility	High 3	Low 1	High 3	Medium 2	Mixed 2	High 3	Low 1
6. Accountability	Low 1	High 3	Low 1	Medium 2	Medium 2	Medium 2	High 3
7. Participation of Leaders	High 3	Low 1	High 3	Low 1	Medium 2	Medium 2	Mixed 2
8. Leadership Democracy	Low 1	High 3	Medium 2	High 3	Low 1	Low 1	High 3
9. Participation of New Leaders	High 3	High 3	Low 1	Medium 2	Medium 2	Low 1	High 3
10. Opposition	Low 1	High 3	Low 1	Low 1	Low 1	Low 1	High 3
11. Democratic Procedures	Mixed 2	Low 1	Low 1	Low 1	Low 1	High 3	Low 1
Total (33)	22	18	18	18	18	23	22

Table 5-2
Representation and Internal Democracy: Summary Rankings

	Total	#High	#Low
1. Hill Health Corporation	23	5	3
2. Block Associations	22	5	3
3. Community School Boards	22	5	5
4. Community Boards	18	4	5
5. Community Task Force	18	3	5
6. Model Cities	18	1*	5
7. Neighborhood Corporations	18	0**	4

*On five tests, Model Cities was ranked "mixed" or "medium."

**On seven tests, Neighborhood Corporations were ranked "mixed" or "medium."

we move from small-scale experiments to more formal neighborhood institutions, significant trade-offs appear to arise between different democratic values. The answer to this puzzle is that the small-scale experiments represent spontaneous, organic expressions of neighborhood cooperation and collective action. On the other hand, the community boards, school boards, and Model Cities are governments-in-miniature created by higher level government for the benefit of neighborhoods. For that reason, the latter are formal and mechanical (there is a uniform design for all neighborhoods, and the design is not created by neighborhood people). Put another way, the small-scale experiments are analogous to informal community organizations, while the assemblies resemble existing, citywide government institutions. As a result, the small-scale experiments have the strengths and weaknesses of spontaneous community organizations. New participants arise in the organization who are dedicated and accessible. At the same time, as in community organizations, there tends to be one-man rule and formal accountability is not emphasized.

Equally, the governments-in-miniature reflect the strengths and weaknesses of existing government institutions. They are governed by established leaders who emphasize formal accountability rather than accessibility, and they generate nonelite participation in the form of protest and disruption.

This analysis suggests that there are two very different approaches to neighborhood government and that neither is likely to satisfy all the tests of representation and internal democracy. The trade-off between democratic values in decentralized government is most clearly revealed in block associations. Only in these face-to-face, grassroots experiments does anything like direct democracy exist, where every resident participates in his small government. But in no other decentralization experiment is there greater one-man rule and less formal accountability and opposition.

6 Neighborhood Politicians: Leadership Styles and Political Efficacy

Blueprints for decentralization implicitly assume the existence of exceptional political leaders. For one thing, the residents' conceptions of neighborhood politicians tends to be plainly heroic.[1] In their view, neighborhood politicians must be dedicated to their experiment even though they are usually not paid for their work. They are expected to have a wide personal knowledge of their community and be easily accessible to their constituents. They must mobilize the community behind the experiment even though the community, if it is a poor one, has had little experience in participation. They must not only carry out an official function as does a councilman, they must also define their role and maintain it in an uncertain environment. Equally, they must not only participate in the work of their neighborhood institution; they must often create that institution, give it shape, and find money to keep it going. They must not only serve the interests of individual residents; they must also represent the interests of "the community" at higher levels of government, although they lack the formal status of elected officials and usually have had no government experience. They must quickly produce tangible successes and benefits for the neighborhood even though no other urban politician from the mayor down has been able to do so. If they are successful in their work, they must not expect promotion to more prestigious political offices. That would be using the community for self-advancement, to "sell out" like all the other politicians. The reward for successful service is continued service. However political their work, neighborhood politicians must not become "political"; they must remain ordinary citizens—"just folks," or risk becoming part of "them"—the existing political establishment.

It is significant, too, that critics of decentralization dwell on perceived weaknesses of neighborhood politicians in making their case against the policy. They suggest that neighborhood leaders are inexperienced, if not incompetent, unrepresentative, and undemocratic. Also, in darker visions, neighborhood leaders are seen as self-serving, unaccountable, racist, and possibly corrupt.[2] In both the romantic ideal and in the nightmare vision, the viability of decentralization thus hinges on the nature and quality of neighborhood politicians.

Who are these neighborhood politicians of whom so much is expected in the quest for neighborhood democracy? What are their backgrounds? What common characteristics do they have? Why did these neighborhood residents become involved in the decentralization experiment? How do they differ in leadership style, political ideology, and political ambition? What kind of political education did they receive in the course of becoming neighborhood leaders? Does their involvement give them a strong sense of political efficacy as advocates of decentralization suggest?

Common Characteristics

Eighty-five neighborhood politicians were interviewed for this study. They were leaders of seven different decentralization experiments. They differed in age, sex, race, ethnicity, and economic background. But they had three characteristics in common: length of residence in their neighborhoods, long-standing community activism, and personal exuberance. In length of residence, 47 percent of the leaders had lived in their neighborhoods for over twenty years, and another 32 percent had lived in the neighborhood between ten and twenty years. With regard to community activism, more than 75 percent of the leaders were members of three or more community organizations (including religious organizations). More than 90 percent of the leaders had been involved in some kind of community work at least five years before the decentralization experiments started. In terms of prior community activism, a difference exists between leaders who represented "new interests" and established community leaders. The former typically were active in church, fraternal, or informal block and tenants groups before becoming involved in the decentralization experiments. The latter typically were past participants or officers in a wide range of major neighborhood organizations.

Vivian Brown, Joe Gonzales, and Pete Fortunato all represent new interests. Mrs. Brown, a block association leader, began her neighborhood involvement working in her church. She later organized a tenants council in her building when the water stopped running and the muggers began. Mr. Gonzales, a member of the Hill Health Corporation, began working in his neighborhood five years ago as a "recruiter" for his church, where he is a lay preacher. The contacts he made canvassing the neighborhood led to occasional participation in the Puerto Rican neighborhood corporation, the Junta. This involvement led, in turn, to active participation in the Hill Health Corporation. Pete Fortunato is now the board chairman of a neighborhood corporation. A lifelong resident of his neighborhood, Pete became involved in a reform campaign in 1970 and later organized a protest against the pollution of a nearby river. As he recalls, "I began to get active about the time the neighborhood corporation was getting going. It was a lucky coincidence. They needed people like me, and I was just beginning to realize what could be done out here."

In all three cases, these "new" neighborhood leaders began with small involvements "close to home" and eventually expanded their involvement and their contacts until they decided to participate actively in the decentralization experiments.

Ernesto Lopez, Henry Peters, and Tom Cider are established community leaders. Like the "new" leaders, their early political careers progressed from limited and parochial participation to involvement in organizations with larger constituencies. Having been recognized as "community leaders," they were asked to participate in numerous other organizations—both those trying to get started and those established organizations wishing to remain influential. According to Lopez, "I've become a kind of one man band. I make a lot of noise in different ways in a lot of different places."

Lopez, a member of his community board, is active in almost every major Puerto Rican organization in the neighborhood. He "sends representatives" to those groups "that I don't have time to work with personally." Peters' involvements also "cover the waterfront," as he puts it. Now a member of Community Board #3, he first became active in the tenants council in his cooperative. "One thing led to another and another," and he is now an officer of the Sixth Avenue Credit Union; a member of the executive committee of the Lower East Side Neighborhood Association; the chairman of the land use committee of the Lower East Side Economic Planning Development Coalition; and the assistant director of a manpower program in a neighborhood multi-service center. Cider, a successful businessman in a white working-class neighborhood, was a founding member of the Ridgewood Community Task Force. He was chosen for the task force by the mayor's Office of Neighborhood Government because he was well known for his work in local organizations: Kiwanis, the YMCA, and the Community Planning Board. He also sponsors a Little League team—the Cider Oilers—a name that is emblazoned on every proudly-worn uniform. Now he is a neighborhood ombudsman: "People call me about potholes. My name is at the top of their minds. They say 'I know you, I've seen you here, I've seen you there'."

For Lopez, Peters, and Cider, neighborhood leadership has become a full-time second job. They are elder statesmen, the people to call about a problem. The more they do in the neighborhood, the more they are asked to do. Their days are filled with a constant round of meetings and telephone calls about community business.

The third shared characteristic of neighborhood politicians is an intangible one. I have called it exuberance. Neighborhood politicians are what James David Barber has termed "active-positive" political leaders.[3] They get involved and stay involved because they have fun doing so. One leader said:

> I go out to meetings most nights of the weeks. You know . . . I come home from work, grab a bite, and then head out again. Many nights I won't get back home to eleven or midnight. Now I say to myself and my wife says too, 'Why do I do all this. . . . I don't need to.' Some of my friends think I'm crazy. They say 'What do you have to show for all this rushing around?' Maybe they're right. Either I'm crazy or I just get a kick out of going to the meetings and seeing the people. It's not that I need something to do either. I like being around my

family, my children, my friends. Still I get itchy to get out in the community and see what's going on. There's always something happening. Maybe it's an unimportant little world . . . all the organizations and meetings, I mean—but, you know, if it's a good sport you're playing, it doesn't matter if you're in the majors or the minors. It's fun, you know, doing all these different things. . . . It's a hell of a lot of fun.

Of course, not all neighborhood politicians are as exuberant as this Community Task Force member. Some get tired of the meetings, problems, and conflicts and others say that active participation "causes you problems at the job and at home. You're burning the candle at both ends." But most are optimists and enthusiasts. They keep participating because, to cite several typical answers, "so much can be done if you work at it"; "it's amazing how much political talent there is out here just waiting to be tapped"; "everybody says there's no community anymore. . . . Well, you get a beautiful feeling of community when you get involved." In most cases, these exuberant words are borne out in action. One block leader runs his basement playroom like a political clubhouse; one Community Task Force member drives around his neighborhood every day to check on the work of pothole-filling crews; one neighborhood corporation member makes regular rounds of neighborhood schools to hear about problems and offer his help; and one member of the Hill Health Corporation spends time at the Health Center every day—"just to keep in touch."

Sources of Participation and Recruitment

Why do neighborhood residents participate in decentralization experiments? And why are certain residents, and not others, recruited to particular experiments? The three common characteristics provide a major part of the explanation. Long-time residence is an obvious source of participation; it creates the desire in leaders to preserve or improve their "home" neighborhood. One block leader said:

I've been living in this neighborhood all my life. One day I was walking home and thinking about all the guys I grew up with who have moved away. I'm about the only one left who grew up here. I decided I wasn't going to let this block go to pot.

Second, the "community revolution" has produced myriad neighborhood organizations that give the activist the opportunity to participate. Given these opportunities, the leaders tend to expand and diversify their involvement. The ladder of participation produces experienced and sometimes prominent neighborhood leaders. It is these leaders who are visible or available: who are recruited for their stature or who are looking for new involvement when decentralization begins. Third, the leaders' exuberance provides the energy that converts concern with neighborhood problems into sustained community activism.

The implication of this analysis is that for neighborhood politicians, participation is not strongly motivated by the desire for economic gain or social status. Also, as will be seen below, political ambition is rarely an important motivation. Money and status are seldom incentives because they are in short supply in decentralization experiments. Participants are unpaid, and their titles do not command particular deference. Participating in the decentralization experiments may reinforce the participant's reputation as a community leader, but many already had that reputation, and others were gaining it independently.

Some neighborhood politicians feel that their participation has an indirect economic and social effect. Tom Cider says that he picks up some business as a result of being a well-known activist in the neighborhood. He also observes that "if you're talking about getting ahead, the business I get from being active is nothing like what I'd get if I spent more time minding the store and less time running around."

William Crocker is a block association president in Brooklyn. He derives two indirect social benefits from his activism. First, he has made new friends on the block since the association started. Second, he feels that he is a leader, that he is making a contribution, "doing what I can to make things a little better." This theme is recurrent. Reacting to the perception that there is nothing anyone can do about urban problems, neighborhood politicians typically feel proud and even significant because as one put it, "We've taken the bull by the horns. Somebody has to try and make things better. . . . Even if you fail trying." Or: "I'm no big politician or anything, but I've stuck my head out. . . . I'm out there fighting . . . not sitting at home complaining. I feel good about that." And further: "In a small way, I'm a leader. I made other people start thinking about what they could do. Nobody did that before."

These feelings of pride and self-esteem have both social and highly personal roots. They are social in that activism gives the resident a social definition as a leader, and he is often greeted with warmth and affection by his neighbors. At the same time, the pride of activism exists regardless of political results (as will be seen below), and it fills a personal need to assert oneself, to make friends, and to "stand up and be counted."

Four Leadership Styles

Neighborhood politicians differ in their sense of purpose and strategy. In terms of purpose, we distinguish between service orientation and power orientation.[4] In a service orientation, the leader's main concern is with specific problems—poor garbage collection, inadequate health facilities, or police patrols, and with specific remedies—increased governmental responsiveness or focused collective action. In a power orientation, the leader's purpose is to gain more political power for neighborhood residents and perhaps work for community control. The power orientation is generalized. The focus is not on specific service problems. The urban problem is defined in terms of the basic structural relationships between city hall and the neighborhoods.

The two orientations are not mutually exclusive. It is possible to be a neighborhood leader who is equally concerned with services and power. However, when the neighborhood leaders were asked the following question, they made a clear choice:

Would you say that you are primarily concerned with service problems—getting better service delivery—or are you primarily concerned with the redistribution of political power—increasing citizen participation and getting more neighborhood control?

In terms of strategy, we distinguish leaders who focus their energies on government from those who focus their energies on the neighborhood. The choice is one of tactics, not purpose. It is a matter of choosing the most promising arena for political leadership and deciding whether government or the community is the more compelling target for political action. Again, it is possible for leaders to pursue both tactics simultaneously. But answers to the following question reveal that neighborhood leaders emphasize one tactic over the other in their political leadership:

As a matter of strategy and priorities, do you feel it is more important to direct your energies to reforming or changing the city government or do you feel it is more important to work at the neighborhood level to develop local capacities and resources?

Leadership style, as it is treated here, is thus an expression of the leader's goals and strategies. In combination, the two sets of contrasting orientations—service versus power, neighborhood versus government—produce four leadership styles. We call them entrepreneurs, ombudsmen, protesters, and community builders. The entrepreneurs are "do-it-yourself" leaders who seek to improve neighborhood services through spontaneous community action. Ombudsmen work to make government respond to specific neighborhood problems. Protesters seek to increase the neighborhood's "say" in government decisions that affect it. At the same time, they fight decisions and policies that they feel have a negative effect on their neighborhood. Community builders seek community control: autonomous neighborhood institutions. Their concern is with the full range of neighborhood problems—broadly defined. There is a strong element of separatism in this approach. The following profiles of neighborhood politicians indicate the characteristic political attitudes and personal traits of the four leadership types.

	Service-Oriented	Power-Oriented
Neighborhood-Oriented	Entrepreneur	Community Builder
Government-Oriented	Ombudsman	Protester

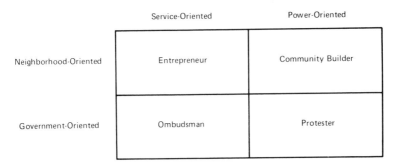

Figure 6-1. Four Styles of Neighborhood Leadership.

The Entrepreneur: "I'm Used to Getting Things Done"

Andy Rotella is a member of the Ridgewood Community Task Force. He is a small contractor who was once a skilled laborer. As a neighborhood leader, he typifies the entrepreneur's attitude toward political leadership and action. He says:

It's incredible how inefficient government is. The government can't do anything unless it sets up an office and hires a million people and has supervisors of supervisors. Even then, it doesn't do anything because there's all this red tape and confusion. You know what a bureaucracy is . . . a place where people sit around all day and look over each other's shoulder. Once you have an office and all those people, no one does anything unless he's told to. He'd be afraid of showing initiative. . . . Might get him in trouble. . . . You know his boss wouldn't like it if people thought they could get along without him. What really bugs me is that once you set up the government office, nobody will go outside. They sit at their desks and answer the telephone. But they don't go out to see what's going on . . . to talk to people and hear about their problems on the spot.

Rotella's remedy is to let able neighborhood residents "run things themselves" because "they'll get things done." He says:

In my book, one good community person is worth 500 government officials. Of course, he has to know what he's doing. . . . He has to be businesslike. . . . He has to have experience in the area . . . like me. . . . I'm used to getting things done. Look, there's lots of people who could do things out here that government couldn't do in a million years. They know the people and the problems and they'll do it for sure. Citizens can do things for themselves that would cost a mint if government tried to do it. That's how I feel—basically we need to get more local people involved on a voluntary basis. . . . You'd get results and cheap, too, that way.

Entrepreneurs thus stress independent action by citizens. They believe that neighborhood residents have special political skills—two of which are common sense and a straightforward technique for "getting things done." They are highly critical of government bureaucracy and its perceived inefficiency. They see themselves as practical people who know how to deal with residents and "get them to work together," as one put it.

The goals of entrepreneurs are concrete, and their tactics depend on personal associations. Doris Brooks, also a block association president, describes her goals in a way that is characteristic of the entrepreneur:

You pick up a well-known problem on the block—say a vacant lot filled with garbage. You get that cleaned up and then you go around and tell people who weren't involved at first what we did. Then you go after another small garbage problem and clean it up. You do this over and over again. Eventually, you have an organization and people believe you and they begin to believe they can get things done themselves.

The Reverend Fred Jones, a board member of the Hill Health Corporation, describes the tactics typically used by entrepreneurs:

It's simple. . . . You pound the pavement, get to know people, go back and see them regularly. You tell them what you're doing and ask them to come to meetings or to take their children over to the center. The only way to organize neighborhood people is to do it personally . . . become someone they know and trust.

In their political ideology entrepreneurs are individualists. They stress individual capabilities and responsibilities. One leader said:

We have been brainwashed to think only the government can help you. That's crap. The only people who can help folks in this neighborhood are the folks themselves. Why? Number one: no one else is going to, and number two: community people will listen to each other but not to outsiders.

Another leader expressed a related theme:

People blame the government for everything. Everything that goes wrong. I think that's copping out. People cause a lot of their own problems and they're the only ones who can solve them. I don't mean that the people on this block are to blame for being poor or having to live in lousy tenements. They are responsible for other things . . . like garbage, fires, drugs, delinquency. Who throws garbage out the window—the government? Who lets Johnny drop out of school and get hooked on junk—the government? No . . . it's the mothers and fathers and the kids themselves. Some say that you can't blame people for things when life's so bad. Well, I blame them for not doing something about those things. The things they could go to work on and change. They could do it if they wanted to. . . . That's where the Neighborhood Corporation comes in . . . to help them get control.

In their view of neighborhood problems, entrepreneurs are practical and specific. They see potholes, particular street gangs, and garbage, not "the crime problem" or "an oppressive system." They pride themselves on knowing what can be done through action and what cannot. One leader said:

We're not trying to be heroes or martyrs or anything like that. So we're not going to try to get the Port Authority to move out of the neighborhood. That would be stupid. We've lost enough already to keep picking impossible fights. So we work on problems that we can take care of . . . visible things . . . small things. I guess we're not ending racism . . . but small things that add up.

As we have seen, entrepreneurs have a low opinion of government bureaucracy. They also have a low opinion of politics and formalized neighborhood organizations. Because they emphasize concrete action and the need to get results, they tend to be critical of meetings, in-fighting, and political bargaining. One leader said:

I quit the community organizations because all they do is talk. I wanted to do something. And I wanted to do it on my own without a bunch of people hanging around.

Another said:

I hate politics. It's all a big con. You have to watch everything they say and do. I wanted to be left alone to really work on our problems and really get into things. That's why I joined the task force.

A third leader said:

There's no way I'd get back into the political game. I've made up my mind on that. You could spend the rest of your life going to meetings.

The Ombudsman: "We're Trying to Make Government Work Right"

Lee Parker runs a small record store in the South Bronx. He also runs a block association and typifies the ombudsman style of neighborhood leadership. He describes his reasons for "getting active" and his goals in the following way:

One morning I was looking out my window and saw the garbagemen come by. One garbageman threw a can over the roof of a car. It bounced on the car and dumped on the street. I said to myself right then . . . this is impossible. We can't live like this. I went to see a friend and we decided to make an experiment . . . see if we could get the government to pick up the garbage. The problem was how to go about it. How do we get information? We went to the Democratic Club. It was election time so they promised us help and jobs. But they didn't come through. Then we went to City Hall. We got sent over to the Office of Neighborhood Government and they helped us get in touch with the right sanitation people. . . . It was a long process. We saw garbage guys downtown and out here. They said, how do we know what you say is true. We could have yelled at them and walked out but we didn't. We said OK we'll prove it. So we took pictures and made reports every day in writing. All together we kept a record of garbage service for a couple of weeks. Then we went back downtown. Meanwhile, we had been keeping in touch with them . . . just so they wouldn't forget who we were. We also got a petition up. People signed if they were angry about the garbage service. Now when we went back to the city people they sat up and listened. We didn't get made at them 'cause everybody else does that and it just gets their back up. They said they'd do this and that and especially send out a sweeper and give us a bulk pickup. We asked when. . . . They said when and they came. We were there to check up. We've done this on other problems. It's like going to school. You learn how to work with the city . . . learn the people and the procedure. Learn when to pressure and when to back off. Learn how to convince them. . . . You know . . . with facts and reports . . . the stuff they understand.The thing is we get better service out here now. We made government do its job. That's all. . . . We're trying to make government work right.

As Parker notes, the ombudsmen seek to improve their neighborhood by improving services. To do this, they focus their energies on government. Ombudsmen all agree that government is the "target you've got to hit." Another ombudsman said:

The [city government's] falling apart. If we let that happen, things are bound to get worse out here. So we try to give them a hand. Of course, we're really putting it to them. But we do it by working with them . . . getting them to see the problems from our point of view.

A third leader said:

The city and Washington have the power and the money so they're the people you have to go to work on. It doesn't make sense to spend your time organizing neighborhood people. They don't have any power and the politicians aren't about to give them any.

The ombudsman's tactics, as Parker's view suggests, are to work the levers of government to the neighborhood's advantage. One leader said, "The neighborhoods are like puppets on a string. City Hall pulls the strings. Now the puppets are learning how the strings work and we're pulling back."

This strategy involves political education, long negotiations with city officials, and persistence. It also involves ingenuity in making contact with the "right" government officials:

We had this problem in one of the schools in Newhallville. The Neighborhood Corporation got involved and was trying to set up a meeting with the mayor to talk things over. Well, you know the mayor doesn't like to meet with large groups of people. He thinks three people's a crowd. So we couldn't get a meeting for a whole group that we couldn't get a meeting for just one of us because there were a lot of different groups involved and we didn't want to go that way. So it looked like there was nothing we could do except picket City Hall and that would have just made the mayor madder at the neighborhood. He's afraid of getting pushed around. Hell, he once climbed out of his window onto the fire escape to get away from a bunch of screaming neighborhood folks in his office. So I decided to use my head. You learn some tricks when you've been at it for a while. I found out where the mayor was going to be the next day. He was going to a groundbreaking. So I went over there and when the mayor was finished shovelling, I walked up beside him and told him my business. He said "Oh, Mrs. ________, it's always nice to see you. You come up and talk seriously and I feel we can get something done." He did help some. . . . Not as much as we'd like, but he made some calls. I've been tracking down people like that ever since. I just sneak up on them.

The ombudsman's political thinking is notable for an individualistic and sometimes atomistic conception of government. This view has two elements. First, the ombudsmen dissent from the view held by many friends that government only listens to neighborhood residents when they are massed in protest groups. For ombudsmen, politics is not a clash of abstract systems, interests, and forces, but a hand-to-hand struggle between resourceful individuals. For this reason, ombudsmen emphasize the importance of learning about government procedures and of developing analytical and negotiating skills. They believe that knowledgeable, flexible, and clever neighborhood leaders will make the greatest impact on government. Second, ombudsmen do not see government as a monolith, but rather as a jigsaw puzzle of agencies and officials. One leader said:

So many.people out here think the mayor's the man. They want to go fight City Hall. You know . . . jump on the mayor's limousine. That's not the way I see it. I figure the mayor doesn't even know what's going on most of the time. The government is run by Tom, Dick, and Harry in one office or another. They're the guys you got to get to know. You got to figure out which guy really makes the decision and work on him. That's the sum of it . . . sort of like solving a puzzle.

In general, ombudsmen believe that government turns out to be a "bunch of pretty confused guys" who often can and must be "educated" about local problems and made responsive to neighborhood demands. In their view of neighborhood problems, ombudsmen, like entrepreneurs, emphasize concrete issues and needs. Describing their neighborhood to a stranger, ombudsmen speak of particular landlords and teachers; they mention a decayed school or an abandoned building where addicts congregate. In their attitude toward politics, ombudsmen stress the importance of shrewd "politicking" with the government but disclaim any interest in politics as a vocation. One ombudsman, who calls himself a "guerrilla in the bureaucratic jungle," described politics as a "waste of time and a bore." This dislike for politics and politicians emerges in interviews with other ombudsmen. They perceive politicians as "self-centered," "full of talk," "out of touch." They say they want to stay out of politics and concentrate on "getting results."

The Protesters: "Power Is the Only Thing City Hall Understands"

Sam Velez is a community board member and the leader of a neighborhood organization in New York. In style and action, he is a protester. He says:

> I've been working in this neighborhood a long time now. I've tried everything—quiet talking, compromise, picketing, and yelling. I find only the protest tactics work. Government won't even listen to you unless you got 150 people yelling under their windows. Try to make appointments with people and follow channels. . . . They change the appointments or don't show up and if that doesn't get you the red tape will. So I've learned how to threaten, and how to scare them. They're all afraid of minority people from the neighborhoods . . . and guilty too. So you just rub their faces into the neighborhood by bringing the neighborhood to them. Remember that power is the only thing government understands . . . and we basically have no power—unless we use our numbers—we got the bodies—or if we use confrontation. If you can't win the way the guys with power play the [political] game, you break the rules. . . . When you don't have power, you do what you can. You huff and you puff, you jump up and down, you come down real hard on the bureaucrats. . . . You make yourself a real pain in the ass. You get your people out to make a lot of noise. You turn their offices into a 3-ring circus. Then they got to do something to get you out. They got to make some concessions.

The goal of protesters is power; in particular, they want a say in decisions affecting the neighborhood. Their tactics, as the above account suggests, are confrontation and disruption.

In their political views, protesters have a well-developed demonology. They see the political process as a battle between inexorable forces: a struggle between "them" and "us." Unlike the entrepreneurs and the ombudsmen, the protesters have an abstract political vision. The protesters believe there is a "system" in society and government that works to "oppress" residents of poor neighborhoods. In general, they have a low opinion of politicians and government officials who they believe are arrogant, cannot be trusted, do not care about neighborhood problems, and only act when they are "up against the wall." One leader said:

> We've been trying for ten years to make the city understand what's going on in

the neighborhood . . . how it has special needs because of the mixture of people . . . how it needs services and housing for the middle-class as well as the poor. Either the city can't understand or it won't understand. Because we're banging our heads on a brick wall. I've decided that the bureaucrats just can't be bothered about us. As long as they don't burn down City Hall, they won't lose their jobs. So there's no reason not to treat us like dirt and give us the runaround when we try to do something. There's not more than a handful of people in the whole municipal building who are worth a damn, who would do something for neighborhood people. . . . How can you be nice and civilized if you have to deal with people like that?

Given these feelings, protesters see little point in trying to work with politicians and officials. One block leader who is a hospital orderly, said, "You have to decide whether you're going to use a scalpel or an axe in dealing with government. From what I've seen, I'll take the axe every time."

In their view of neighborhood problems, the protesters' vision again is highly generalized. They do not talk about specific service problems but about education, housing decay, the insensitivity of public employees, and the failure of government. If they are nonwhite, they talk about racist policemen and politicians—indeed racist government and racist society. If they are white, they talk about the way their neighborhood has been forgotten and left to decline. They complain that their neighborhood is becoming a slum and point to nearby nonwhite areas. White or black, protesters see a seamless web of problems and focus on specific issues only when the issues are sufficiently dramatic to symbolize the general condition of the neighborhood. Protesters say they scorn politics as a possible career because they believe that politicians are part of an "inhuman," "oppressive," and "corrupt" system. They feel the only reason to go into politics would be for money or prestige. But that would be "selling out," becoming part of "them."

At the same time, they believe their neighborhoods or ethnic groups lack "real" representation—by people "who know and care"—in larger political institutions, and this feeling impels them toward the political arena. Thus, the protesters have conflicting feelings toward political life. Should they try to give the neighborhood a badly needed voice in government if that means dealing with a discredited political system?

The Community Builder: "If We Want to Run Our Own Lives, We Have to Build Our Own Institutions."[a]

Lewis Green is a community school board member on New York's Lower East Side. He's the director of a community preschool day care center and exhibits the leadership style and attitudes of the community builder. He says:

[a]Because few neighborhood leaders exhibit the "community builder" style of political leadership, this profile rests on a small number of long interviews. The reasons for the small number of community builders will be discussed below.

As far as I'm concerned, I'd like to go back to 'separate but equal.' Integration is a nice idea but it won't work. The white power structure won't let black people into the system and all we get for our trouble is the crumbs from the table. That's why the neighborhood organizations and all other kinds of participation are a fraud. We're all fighting for the few crumbs the white man gives us. All we do is fight among ourselves . . . and for what? It's like you put rats in a hole . . . if they don't get any food, they'll eat hair . . . each other's hair . .,. So I don't see any point in working with City Hall or working within the system. We got to do it ourselves. Run our own schools, build our own housing, make our own plans. If we want to run our own lives, we have to build our own institutions. You can call me a separatist if you want. That's O.K. It's the only way. The only power we have is out here on the streets. We have to put it together . . . do our own thing for ourselves all the government programs in the world don't mean shit. We got to solve our problems right here with our own brains and muscle.

This view is obviously that of a minority group member. But the same view is expressed without the emphasis on racial conflict by two white community builders. These are white leaders who want to control their own schools and police and the kind of housing that is built in their neighborhood. They want the government to "get off our backs" and, as Lewis Green put it, "let us run our own lives."

The goal of the community builder thus is local development and self-determination. If this means separatism, so be it. The strategy of the community builder is clear in theory, uncertain in practice. In principle, it entails institution-building through collective action and individual initiative. In practice, it involves discussions of "economic development," housing corporations, and community control of schools. Where to begin? Where to find resources for community development? These are questions that community builders answer vaguely if at all.

In their political vision, the community builders interviewed see a clear dichotomy between "them"—the city government, and "us"—the neighborhood. They see the "city," the political system, as implacably hostile to the neighborhood. By contrast, they see the neighborhood and neighborhood people as the only source of positive political action.

In their view of neighborhood problems, community builders, like protesters, see a complex interaction of social and economic troubles. At the heart of the problem, they believe, is the neighborhood's lack of power, and related to that its lack of resources. One leader said: "You can't make an omelette if you don't have any eggs."

In their view of political life, community builders, again like protesters, see the "political game" as a sellout and, more important, a waste of time. But there is no ambivalence in the community builder's view of politics as a vocation. They view political involvement as a distraction from the "real work" of community organizing and institution-building. As one put it, "I can't be bothered with that shucking and jiving. I'll leave that to the fellas with pretty faces who want to get their pictures taken."

The Distribution of Leadership Styles

It is significant that neighborhood politicians differ in their leadership styles, for different styles lead to different strategies and, as will be seen below, to different "political" futures. However, if neighborhood leaders were divided evenly among the four styles, we might conclude that the choice between styles is relatively random, a matter of subtle accentuation that does not tell us much about political leadership in decentralization experiments. For this reason, it is significant that the four styles were far from evenly distributed in the sample of eight-five leaders. In fact, two leadership types–entrepreneur and ombudsman–were dominant. Taken together they constituted 71 percent of the sample; 39 percent entrepreneurs and 32 percent ombudsmen. In contrast, only 22 percent of the neighborhood leaders were protesters, and 7 percent community builders. These distributions obtained for both sexes and among different racial, age, and occupational groups. This finding indicates that most decentralization leaders are service-oriented, have an individualistic vision of government and politics, and take a concrete view of neighborhood problems. In short, they are pragmatic, nonideological leaders who like to solve concrete problems.

What explains this distribution of leadership styles? Why do decentralization experiments produce this kind of leadership? The answer lies in the nature of the decentralization experiments and in the social background of the neighborhood leaders. For one thing, leaders of decentralization experiments feel they must produce results quickly. No longer having to fight city hall for participation, they must now make their own experiments work. One leader said, "The tables have been turned. We used to build our support by beating up on the government. Now we have to deliver the goods ourselves. We have to put up or shut up." The result is that leaders stress service needs and tangible, visible benefits. Further, neighborhood politicians tend to be "moderate" and pragmatic for reasons of background and experience. Seventy-nine percent of neighborhood politicians were professionals, businessmen, government employees, white-collar workers, and established leaders of community organizations. They have had some success in the social and economic "system" and see themselves as tough-minded and realistic, as "responsible" leaders, "negotiators," people who "get things done." This self-image militates against political radicalism and angry rhetoric. These leaders were also long-time neighborhood residents with broad experience in neighborhood organizations. Whatever their attitudes to the city hall "establishment," they tended to be "established" members of their small communities–people with roots.

Recruitment to Decentralization Experiments

Why do particular leaders participate in particular experiments? There are two closely related answers. First, experiments have different leadership needs, and second, individual leaders are attracted to the kind of leadership role for which their previous political experience prepared them. Thus, recruitment to decentralization experiments is a process of matching organizational needs with personal skills and predispositions.

Most of the experiments have distinctive purposes and orientations. Block associations and the Hill Health Corporation have obvious entrepreneurial orientations. The Community Task Force has a clear ombudsman orientation. On the other hand, community boards, as institutionalized advocates of neighborhood interests and critics of government policy, have a structural bias towards protest; and in the New Haven Model Cities program, where residents have long fought for a greater role in decisionmaking, there is also a natural tendency toward protest.

Significantly, there is a close fit between the orientation of the decentralization experiments and the leadership styles of the neighborhood politicians. Sixty percent of the block association leaders were "entrepreneurs," as were 88 percent of the Hill Health Corporation leaders. While 54 percent of the Community Task Force members were ombudsmen, 44 percent of the Model Cities leaders and 50 percent of the community board members were protesters. This evidence shows clearly that the structural attributes of the experiments influence the recruitment of leaders and the character of political leadership.

The further question is: what kind of people become "entrepreneurs," "ombudsmen," "protesters," or "community builders." My argument is that leadership style reflects the resident's occupation and prior political experience. Many entrepreneurs in politics are also entrepreneurs in business or the professions. Over 80 percent of the entrepreneurs were small businessmen, lawyers, clergymen, and other local professionals. Their career backgrounds give then a distinctive orientation toward individual action and problem-solving. Two examples illustrate this point. Harry Parker is a black businessman who worked his way from factory employment to ownership of a small fabricating plant. As a founder of the Hill Health Corporation, he has applied the techniques learned in his daily life: "no-nonsense" organization, "getting out a product." The Reverend Allen Peters, a minister and leader of one of the New Haven neighborhood corporations, practices politics in the same way he conducts his pastoral duties: through home visits and block-by-block canvassing. He believes that in his community activism he is doing what he knows how to do best: "make contact with people and persuade them to get involved."

Among the "ombudsmen," more than 60 percent were government employees, professionals (lawyers, school teachers, and a librarian), and leaders of community organizations. The identifying characteristic is that they are used to working *in* large bureaucracies and, in many cases, *with* government bureaucracies. Their careers have provided an education in administrative politics. Robert Bonds is the librarian of a public library in Queens and a member of the Community Task Force. In his words, he has been "bucking the city bureaucracy for a long time. After a while, you learn how to deal with the people downtown. You find out who to talk to and how to talk to them." As a Community Task Force member, he is trying to apply the same techniques to getting the city bureaucracy to respond to air pollution problems in the neighborhood. Joe Brown is the leader of the Dixwell Neighborhood Corporation and an ombudsman. As an alderman he gained valuable political experience and contacts that enabled him to handle neighborhood case work. Now he is doing the same job he used to do as a political official; only now, as he puts it, he is "wearing a different hat." A third ombudsman, Ed Harris, is also the leader of a neighborhood corporation. His job, as he sees it, is to make the city's antipoverty agency, Community Progress Inc., more responsive to the neighborhood. As a former employee of CPI, he received on-the-job training in dealing with city government.

The leadership style of neighborhood politicians is also shaped by prior political experience. James David Barber has stressed the importance of a politician's "first independent political success" in the formation of his leadership style.[5] Neighborhood politicians, no less than presidents, receive a political education, the lessons of which they tend to apply in new situations over and over again. With the neighborhood politician, it is not only the first political success that matters. It is the repetition of tactics and techniques, the repeated choice of problems appropriate to the tactics, and the forming of political habits that forge a distinctive leadership style.

Mrs. Mary Johnson is a neighborhood corporation leader who has developed her ombudsman style over twenty years of dealing with city government. Her first involvement was in the tenants' council of her housing project. Threatened with eviction, she established a "working relationship" with the Housing Authority and won concessions. Later, she became president of her local P.T.A. and, in her words, "learned to talk to the Board of Education people." She moved to a new neighborhood and became chairman of a new P.T.A. In that role, she "got to know the mayor, and he got to know us. We cooperated with him, and he cooperated with us." Her tactic was to establish contact with public officials and form a "working relationship" for the benefit of the neighborhood. This she applied repeatedly in different organizations: first, in a neighborhood organization in Newhallville, then in the neighborhood corporation.

John Morales is a protester and has always been one. A community board member, he began his career as a neighborhood activist protesting housing conditions. He "screamed and yelled and, when nothing happened, [he] screamed and yelled some more." In his own words, he has been "screaming and yelling" ever since. He is now a member of various neighborhood organizations and, in each, he sticks to his political habits. He says: "I've learned a simple lesson. The power structure only listens when you turn the noise up so loud they can't do anything else. That's the way it is."

The Political Future of Neighborhood Leaders

Moynihan has argued that a major impact of the community action program was the development of indigenous political leadership.[6] Indeed, the political justification of decentralization is that it produces leaders who will mobilize the neighborhood and articulate the neighborhood's interests in wider political arenas. To what extent do the neighborhood leaders fulfill or show promise of fulfilling these expectations? In the first place, the political future of neighborhood politicians depends on leadership style. Entrepreneurs, for example, have a different sense of their role and of political life than protestors. However, none of the four leadership types is strongly inclined towards a career in elective politics. The entrepreneurs are antipolitical; they want to get "something done" at the street level and cannot be bothered with the vagaries of political life. Ombudsmen concentrate on specific neighborhood problems and believe that government bureaucracies are the most important targets of neighborhood action. The protesters scorn politics as a fraud, but some nevertheless believe that neighborhood leaders might fight for a voice in the political "system." If that means elective politics, so be it. Finally, the community builders are too busy mobilizing neighborhood resources and energies to worry about political office-holding. Thus, aside from some protesters, neighborhood leaders are unlikely to pursue a political career: they have no plans to advance neighborhood interests through political office holding. On the other hand, many ombudsmen have received an ideal preparation for higher administrative posts in government. And some protesters would accept a higher-level job in city government as a way of making the bureaucracy more representative, as a way of "getting some black faces in City Hall."

The second element of the political justification of decentralization is that neighborhood leaders will mobilize neighborhood resources and stimulate collective action at the local level. To what extent do neighborhood leaders fulfill this expectation? Here leadership style is decisive. Of the four leadership styles, only the entrepreneurs and the community builders work to mobilize neighborhood resources in a sustained fashion. The ombudsmen work mainly with government, and protesters "mobilize their troops" only sporadically for demonstrations against the government. As mobilizers of neighborhood resources, the entrepreneurs' role is limited by its service orientation, and the community builders' role is prospective and often wishful. More precisely, because entrepreneurs focus on collective self-help projects rather than on increased political power, they typically mobilize a limited constituency for sharply defined purposes. They stimulate collective action, but their success is often dependent on the narrow focus of that action. By contrast, community builders seek to mobilize the neighborhood in a more general and ambitious way. They want to develop local political power, and they address broad problems such as housing and economic development. However, given the neighborhood's limited resources and the scope of neighborhood problems, community builders seek an intrinsically difficult form of neighborhood mobilization.

In sum, to the extent that neighborhood experiments and their leaders remain service-oriented, decentralization is likely to generate only a narrow-gauged mobilization of neighborhood resources.

Political Leadership and Political Efficiency

Decentralization is also launched in the hope of increasing neighborhood residents' sense of political efficacy and, conversely, of reducing their feelings of powerlessness. This is the point of bringing government "closer to the people," of including neighborhood residents in government. Does decentralization have this impact in practice? We have no way of knowing what impact decentralization has on the ordinary neighborhood resident. Nor is it obvious that the litmus test of decentralization should be a universal change of political attitudes in the neighborhood. That may be asking too much of any political innovation—especially when it has just begun. However, we can determine whether decentralization gives the leaders of the various experiments a strong sense of political efficacy. To measure their sense of political efficacy, we asked the eighty-five neighborhood politicians the following questions:

1. Working in this program, do you feel that you have a voice, a "say" in government?
2. Do you feel that your work in this program has a real impact on the way government delivers services in the neighborhood?
3. Do you feel that your work on this program has real impact on conditions in the neighborhood?
4. Having worked in this program, do you feel that citizens working together can fight City Hall—make government more responsive to the needs of the neighborhood?
5. Having worked in this program, do you feel more hopeful that there are ways to solve problems in your neighborhood?

In evaluating the leaders' responses to these tests of political efficacy, we must keep two considerations in mind. First, political leaders already have a personal sense of efficacy. They are exuberant; they have fun doing neighborhood work; they take pride in the fact that they are trying to improve their neighborhood, that they have decided to "stand up and be counted." Second, various studies have shown that political activists, in general, have a strong sense of political efficacy.[7] For these reasons, we would expect all neighborhood leaders to score high on the tests of political efficacy and would find it particularly significant if many leaders had low scores. In fact, many neighborhood leaders did score low on the tests of political efficacy. Scoring one point for a "yes" answer and a half point for a "somewhat," "sometimes," or a "yes and no" answer, we have a nine point scale of political efficacy: 1, 1.5, 2, 2.5 . . . 9.[8] In all, 31 percent of the leaders had a low sense of efficacy (3 points and below), and 48 percent of the leaders scored 5 or less on the nine-point scale. These leaders gave "yes" answers to no more than three of the questions on political efficacy. At the other end of the scale, 20 percent of the leaders answered "yes" to all five questions and 36 percent had a score of 8 or higher.

This distribution of political efficacy scores permits one simple conclusion: decentralization does not automatically produce a strong sense of political efficacy among participants in neighborhood experiments. But what explains the distribution of efficacy scores? Why did some leaders score high and others low when the findings show that differences in political efficacy cannot be explained by differences in race, age, occupation, or length of residence in the neighborhood? The answer is that political efficacy varies with leadership style and experiment—especially the latter. Fifty-eight percent of the entrepreneurs scored 8 or higher, as did 40 percent of the ombudsmen. In contrast, 70 percent of the protesters scored 3 or lower as did 38 percent of the community builders. Leadership style is, therefore, a broad determinant of political efficacy. But, as we have seen, leadership style is shaped by the orientation of the decentralization experiment. And, indeed, the clearest differences in political efficacy existed between leaders of different experiments. Forty-seven percent of the block association leaders had an efficacy score of 9, and 63 percent had a score of 8 or higher. Over 60 percent of the Community Task Force leaders had a score of 8 or higher. Fifty-six percent of the Hill Health Corporation leaders had a score of 9, and all the leaders had a score of 8 or better. In contrast, 90 percent of the community board leaders scored 3 or less; 67 percent of the Model Cities leaders scored 3 or less; and 75 percent of the community school board members scored 5 or less. The leadership of neighborhood corporations had the most irregular pattern of political efficacy, the scores being distributed across the scale. However, 47 percent of the neighborhood corporation leaders scored 3 or less on the efficacy scale. The average political efficacy score for leaders are shown in Table 6-1. The average scores for each experiment fall into three clusters. In three experiments, Model Cities, community boards, and the community school boards, leaders clearly had a low sense of political efficacy; while in block associations, the Community Task Force, and the Hill Health

Table 6-1
Political Efficacy by Experiment—Average Score

Hill Neighborhood Corporation	8.5
Community Task Force	7.7
Block Associations	7.7
Neighborhood Corporations	4.9
Community School Boards	3.6
Community Boards	3.0
Model Cities	2.9

Corporation the scores were very high. In one experiment, the neighborhood corporation, the leaders' efficacy fell right in the middle of the spectrum. This evidence suggests two important conclusions. First, the neighborhood leaders' sense of political efficacy is not strongly related to the extent of decentralization in their experiments (see Table 6-2). The disparity between the two rankings is great in four cases and, significantly, two of the experiments whose leaders rank highest on the political efficacy scale have little formal power. Second, and more important, the political efficacy scores are directly related to the rankings of the experiments on initiatives and impacts (see Table 6-3). The fit between efficacy and impact is almost perfect and shows that neighborhood leaders judge "participation" not in terms of the process of participation or the opportunity to participate, but in terms of the concrete results of participation.[9] For neighborhood residents, participation is not an end in itself, an honor, or a noble exercise in citizenship; it is an instrument for solving problems, for improving neighborhood conditions quickly and visibly. Simply put, the worth of participation is its "cash value" at the street level.

Table 6-2
Political Efficacy and Degree of Decentralization

Experiment	Political Efficacy Ranking	Ranking on Decentralization Scale
Hill Neighborhood Corporation	1	2
Community Task Force	2	5
Block Associations	2	7
Neighborhood Corporations	4	3
Community School Boards	5	1
Community Boards	6	6
Model Cities	7	4

Table 6-3
Political Efficacy and Neighborhood Impact

Experiment	Political Efficacy Ranking	Impact Ranking
Hill Neighborhood Corporation	1	1
Community Task Force	2	2
Block Associations	2	3
Neighborhood Corporations	4	4
Community School Boards	5	5
Community Boards	6	7
Model Cities	7	6

This thesis is reinforced by the anomalous political efficacy scores in the different experiments. For example, the average efficacy score for Community Task Force leaders was high, but one leader had a low score. He was the ombudsman in charge of getting the city to move on air pollution problems in the neighborhood. He had little success: "I'm getting the run-around," he says. "All we do is write letters back and forth . . . and then nothing happens."

The average efficacy score for school board members was low, but one leader, Ray Espada, had a score of 9. He was concerned that no procedures existed in his school district for evaluating teacher performance, so he designed guidelines for evaluating teachers and, after much maneuvering, got it accepted by parents, teachers, and other school board members. He says: "I focused on a small problem . . . No one was doing anything about it, so it was a wide open issue. I got the plan on the table, forced people to deal with it and steered it through . . . I feel I really got something done . . . I stuck with it all the way."

As we have seen, the leaders of neighborhood corporations had diverse efficacy scores. These differences are easily explained. Some leaders, like the leaders of the Newhallville Corporation, have a long record of winning small concessions from the city government. They have lobbied successfully to get a new school built, to shape the urban renewal plan in their neighborhood and to block a proposed suburban-commuter transportation project which would run through their neighborhood. By contrast, the leaders of the Wooster Square Corporation have had difficulty "even getting the organization off the ground." They cannot get people to serve on the board of directors, and they feel they have been discriminated against by city and state poverty agencies in the annual allocation of funds. They had a very low sense of political efficacy.

Political Education and Political Efficacy

Neighborhood leaders do not develop a strong sense of political efficacy overnight. They gain it through the experience of making decisions and grappling with problems, and, in so doing, they learn how to be effective and how to take advantage of opportunities and available resources. The leaders with the strongest sense of political efficacy have learned two simple lessons in the course of their political education. The first lesson is to pick "winning issues." As one leader said: "There are a million problems out here. Most of the them are beyond my reach. What I try to do is spot the issue that I've got enough firepower to hit. I started out with a shotgun approach, but that's stupid. You hit everything and nothing. Now I don't shoot until I know I'm gonna hit the target."

The second lesson learned by these neighborhood leaders is that you develop political resources by delivering visible service to neighborhood residents. Another leader said:

> When I started out, I frankly didn't know what to do or how to get things done. I thought maybe you hold a lot of meetings and work out a program that covers everything. Or maybe you try to build alliances with all sorts of organizations. Or make plans for the neighborhood. But I just couldn't get a handle on things thinking like this . . . And no one else was much interested in meetings, plans, or big ideas for new programs . . . I learned how you put it together one day by accident. I got some money for the local Police Athletic League . . . Just like that, they started taking us seriously. They wanted to do business. They came to us for help. Just because I delivered the goods . . . pretty small ones. I did this a couple of more times. I told people I'd do something and I did it and then we moved on to something else. Pretty soon the word got around . . . People believed I could deliver . . . that I wasn't just full of crap. Some people now think I can make miracles. That's my political power . . . my laundry ticket, you might say.

Part III
Patterns of Neighborhood Democracy: Some Explanations

7 The Political Economy of Decentralization

Having examined the seven experiments we can now assess the overall impact of these innovations in decentralization. Adopting a street-level perspective, we ask; what returns do neighborhood leaders get from their investment in decentralization? And what explains the relationship between investment and impact? Taken together, the seven experiments do not reveal any clear-cut verdict on decentralization. None has fulfilled all the hopes of decentralization advocates. None has totally failed. Even the most troubled experiment has produced some measure of responsiveness or has provided a forum for articulating neighborhood interests and needs. It is important to emphasize, too, that decentralization experiments have several goals, and the achievement of one goal does not guarantee success with the others. Some experiments have a strong impact on neighborhood problems but do not provide strong representation and internal democracy. Nor does progress in one aspect of internal democracy mean progress in other aspects. The leadership of one experiment may be accountable to nonleaders, but not easily accessible to them. Strong representation of "new interests" does not necessarily follow from strong "social representation."

At the same time, certain outputs are strongly related. The sense of political efficacy possessed by neighborhood leaders is a function of the impacts that these experiments have on neighborhood problems. The greater the impact, the greater the sense of political efficacy. In addition, impacts also affect leadership participation. The greater the impact, the stronger and more sustained the leaders' participation.

A Structural Explanation

What accounts for these patterns of innovation and impact? The explanation offered here focuses on the structural characteristics of decentralization experiments. Structural similarities as well as differences enter into the explanation. Let us first consider two common characteristics: (1) Leaders in decentralization are suddenly in the position of having some power and authority and the heavy responsibility of "delivering the goods" to their constituents and (2) almost no neighborhood leaders are paid for their work. The effect of the first characteristic is to make neighborhood leaders service-oriented, concerned with concrete and visible benefits. The second characteristic has a strong effect on the recruitment of leaders. Because the poor and "working poor" lack the personal resources for the "voluntary altruism" required by decentralization, middle-class residents dominate the experiments. The leaders are professionals, small businessmen, teachers, and housewives, who have the time to participate. Many are employed by existing community organizations and are, therefore, professional neighborhood activists. Thus, the politics of neighborhood government are no different from politics at any other level. Participation depends on personal resources. This pattern is clearly manifest in the experience of the community school boards where voting turnout was lowest in the poorest neighborhoods, and the incidence of bitter conflict and corruption was highest.

The most obvious and important finding is that different experiments produce different outcomes. While acknowledging that each experiment is in some sense unique (existing in one place at one time), my argument is that decentralization experiments take several basic forms and that these forms powerfully shape the outcome of decentralization.[1]

The question becomes: What structures and political arrangements are most conducive to achieving the goals of decentralization? We can immediately give one negative answer to this question. That is, the degree of decentralization does not determine the level of impact. This is clearly demonstrated by the success of block associations and the Community Task Force and the difficulties experienced by Model Cities and the community school boards.

If the degree of local power is not the crucial structural variable, what is? In terms of representation and internal democracy, the difference between informal, small-scale structures and formal, neighborhoodwide ones is central. The former provide strong representation of new interests, accessibility, and leadership participation while the latter do not. The formal comprehensive experiments provide strong accountability, leadership democracy, and participation of nonleaders; the informal, small-scale experiments do not. Thus we have two structural variables (informal-formal, small-scale-neighborhoodwide) that appear to explain part of the outcome of decentralization. But the explanation is obviously incomplete. It only covers one outcome of decentralization, and it is not really an explanation at all. To explain the politics and impacts of decentralization, we need to know why certain structures produce certain results, not simply that they do so.

In what follows, we develop two explanatory propositions about successful institution-building in urban neighborhoods: (1) The outcome of decentralization is a function of the resources the experiments possess relative to: (a) the difficulty of the tasks they perform and (b) the magnitude of the political and organizational costs they bear. (2) To persuade citizens to invest in decentralization, it is necessary that the rewards of such action be greater than the personal costs. Serious participation is likely to occur only when neighborhood innovations offer visible rewards and work to solve concrete problems.[2]

Task Orientation

The work of the experiments is defined by their fundamental purpose. This is an obvious but not empty assertion. The community school boards had to deal with the full range of educational and administrative issues that arise in their schools. Otherwise they could not attempt to "govern" education in any meaningful sense. The community boards must deal with a great number of planning and development issues if they are to serve as a community forum and sounding board. Similarly, Model Cities and neighborhood corporations have a diffuse agenda created by the breadth of their mandate. By contrast, the work of the Community Task Force and the Hill Health Corporation is focused because their mandates are focused: the experiments were designed to deal with a specific and bounded set of service problems.

Information Costs

A diffuse mandate produces another effect. The more diffuse the tasks of decentralization the greater are the costs of getting information about relevant problems and programs.[3] The leaders of community boards and Model Cities are constantly involved in a frustrating search for information about government decisions, plans, and reports or about the basic characteristics of neighborhood problems. One community board member said: "We can't plan or make decisions if we can't find out what's going on . . . but we have to chase all over the city to learn what's happening on our doorstep. It's a ridiculous scavenger hunt." Similarly, many of the neighborhood corporations set out to develop broad-gauged plans for their neighborhoods and wound up mired in data collection. Some, despite an expensive investment of time and energy, were unable to develop even a crude portrait of relevant issues and problems. Information costs in the community school boards are high for a different reason: there is too much information. School board members complain that they are swamped by memos, reports, regulations. One said: "You ought to see what comes across my desk each week. Nobody could keep up with it . . . it's impossible. We have so much to learn. We need to get down to the real issues, but we spend all our time fighting through the paper."

In contrast, leaders of the small-scale experiments do not have this problem. Block associations, says one leader, focus on what "we can see and feel." The Community Task Force leaders deal with common, easily understood service problems, and the Health Corporation leaders supervise visible health services. These leaders gain information about the program from watching what goes on in the clinic and by talking to doctors, nurses, and patients. The work of the personnel and budget committees is also highly tangible. The personnel committee gets the information it needs interviewing prospective candidates. The finance committee deals mainly with decision-relevant information: should *x* service be increased, is there enough money for another nurse.

Choice

Choice is another important dimension of task orientation. At one extreme, the community school boards have little choice about what tasks they perform. Their task is defined by established educational practices, and existing administrative rules and routines; and their agenda is limited by law and union contract. At the other extreme, block associations have no fixed mandate or agenda. Block leaders can pick whatever tasks they find appropriate to their skills and resources. The leaders of the Hill Health Corporation also have considerable flexibility in setting their agenda, for the experiment is neither tied directly to a government bureaucracy nor does it have to adjust to preexisting rules and routines. This flexibility is an important ingredient in any decentralization experiment. If their agenda is flexible, neighborhood leaders can devise their own strategy and search for winning issues. Without flexibility, the neighborhood position is both reactive and constrained.

In summary, the tasks of decentralization differ from one experiment to another. The more diffuse the tasks of decentralization the more difficult it will be for the experiment to have an impact on neighborhood problems. Further, the more inflexible the tasks of decentralization, the more difficult it will be for the experiment to have an impact.

Degree of Difficulty

The task orientation of decentralization experiments has one further dimension. Simply, some urban problems are easier to solve than others. At one extreme, no one knows how to solve the education problem in low-income suburban schools. No one knows what solutions will work: more or different teachers, more or different compensatory programs, more integration, etc. Yet the success of the community school boards depends ultimately on their ability to solve this inherently complex problem. Neighborhood corporations and Model Cities desire to have an impact on housing, education, and economic development in their neighborhoods, and this leads them into similarly complex and difficult problems. The problems of housing and economic development are as difficult as those of education, but for different reasons: they are resource problems and their solution requires a large capital investment. By contrast, many of the problems attacked by block associations and the Community Task Force are uncomplicated, and their solution is clear cut. Cleaning up a block, getting a pothole filled, painting a house are "low-budget" tasks. Most of the ombudsman tasks that require a smooth-working relationship with city departments have a simple solution once that relationship is established. And the initial investment involved in setting up those relationships does not require large financial resources. It is obvious but important that the more complex the problems the more difficult it will be for decentralization experiments to have an impact. For if the sense of political efficiency depends on concrete impacts, decentralization experiments must have winning issues if they are to develop. If the experiments must deal only with insoluble problems for which they lack adequate resources, they are certain to fail.

The implication here is not that decentralization experiments should be concerned only with simple problems that can be easily solved. The implication is that an experiment that cannot possibly meet its objectives is worse than no decentralization experiment at all. The further implication is that if complex, capital-intensive problems are to be attacked, decentralization experiments must have the resources required to convert investment into impact. Otherwise, the experiment is an exercise in "planned failure."

Organizational Costs of Decentralization

Decentralization experiments can be structured in different ways to accomplish their tasks. But different structural designs carry with them different organizational costs. The greater the costs the more difficult it is for decentralization experiments to have an impact and the more resources are needed to convert investment by neighborhood leaders into impact on neighborhood problems.

Costs of Democracy

One important structural variable has already been discussed: the distinction between formal and informal organization—especially in terms of democratic procedure. It is clear that formal democracy is a costly process that takes time and energy.[4] One neighborhood leader said, "It seems like you have to choose where to put your energies, into meetings or into programs and action. Of course, you should really do both—but you don't have enough time. It got so we were having almost nightly meetings at the corporation. We were real democrats . . . we had great participation, but that's all we did. We didn't get anything accomplished."

The trade-off between investment in political action and formal democracy applies in most of the decentralization experiments. The experiments designed as formal assemblies pay a high price to maintain their democratic process. The community boards, as we have seen, tend to become debating societies in the course of functioning as a community forum. Many community school board members complain that the meetings and the "process" drain away all their time and energy. To a lesser extent, the leaders in Model Cities with its complicated system of participation are hard pressed to make the process work at all. By contrast, those block associations characterized by one-man leadership focus their energies directly on neighborhood problems. So do the leaders of the Community Task Force who spend little of their time in meetings and deliberations. To a lesser extent, the Hill Health Corporation reduces the costs of formal democracy by relying on strong leadership and on the personnel and finance committees. In general, the more formal the democratic process, the greater the costs borne by decentralization experiments—and the more time and energy are required to convert investment into impact. The implication of this analysis is *not* that it is a mistake for neighborhood institutions to be democratic. The implication is that it is crucial to realize that democracy is not only a virtue but a burden and that a formal experiment in neighborhood democracy lacking substantial resources is likely to produce the frustrated reaction: "all we do is talk."

Economies of Scale

A second important structural variable has also been discussed: the distinction between small-area and neighborhoodwide constituencies. This variable has a strong effect on the organizational costs of decentralization. The larger the community coalition, the more community conflicts and cleavages are likely to arise—and the more time it is likely to take the experiment to take action. The difficulty of aggregating and articulating diverse interests is obvious in three neighborhoodwide assemblies: community boards, Model Cities, and community school boards. In contrast, block associations, the Community Task Force, and the Hill Health Corporation deal with limited constituencies that tend to articulate similar if not common needs and interests. The similarity of interests exists in these cases because the tasks of the experiments are highly focused: on one small block, on particular kinds of service problems, and on childrens' health needs. Ironically, some neighborhood corporations deal with a small and manageable constituency because they have shallow roots in the community. If only fifty or a hundred people participate in the corporation, the experiments end up operating on roughly the same scale as the intentionally small-scale block associations.

The Problem of Size in Decisionmaking

The larger the representative body that governs the experiment, the greater the organizational costs of decisionmaking. More precisely, the greater the number of representatives, the more time it will take to reach agreement and the more conflicting interests will exist that have to be accommodated.[5] It is obvious that a decisionmaking group of three is likely to do its business more easily than a group of 200. Even in less extreme cases, the size principle applies. For example, the community boards are clearly unwieldy at fifty members. With that many interests and indeed seats at the conference table, it is hard to do much else but debate. In Model Cities, there are two separate representative bodies that have more than twenty-four members each. The community school boards formally have only nine members, but related representative groups such as advisory councils, parent-teacher associations, and teacher unions swell the number of effective participants dramatically. Informal experiments avoid the problems of size in decisionmaking in two ways. First, the block associations and Community Task Force have a small active leadership group of between five and ten residents. Second the Hill Health Corporation, as we have seen, relies on the president, and on the two small task-oriented committees.

There is an obvious need here to distinguish between formal and informal organizations. Most of the experiments produce a small informal leadership group. What is important is that formal organization places a constraint on informal leadership. Where large representative bodies are established, the rank and file members refuse to let officers "run the show." And to the extent that broad-level participation and representation are considered important, the movement to small, informal leadership undermines these democratic "virtues."[6] In sum, large decisionmaking bodies force neighborhood leaders into a routine of "meetings, meetings, and more meetings."

The size of the decisionmaking body is particularly important in experiments like the community boards where the neighborhood needs to present a united format in lobbying for or protesting against government policies. The logic of advisory boards is such that either internal divisions or the inability to reach strong and clear positions make this form of participation ineffectual.

The Costs of Entanglement

A fourth structural variable concerns the relationship between city government and neighborhood experiments. Are the neighborhood structures independent of city government, completely dependent on them, or are the two closely intertwined? For several reasons, the more dependent or intertwined the neighborhood institutions, the higher the costs of decisionmaking at the local level. The idea of "entangling alliances" is a familiar one in American politics.[7] In decentralization experiments, the problem is one of entanglements that may produce constant friction if not open conflict. When the neighborhood and city structures are closely intertwined, problems of authority, responsibility and communications result. In general, neighborhood leaders wish to be autonomous, and the more they have to work within the rules and routines and under the instruction of city government, the more constrained and resentful they feel. These frictions and conflicts appear most clearly in the Model Cities program, the neighborhood corporations, and the community school boards–all experiments that are either intertwined with or dependent on city government.

The authority problem is both substantive and symbolic. Consider the community school boards. When the city and the neighborhoods share power in many areas of governance, substantive disagreements are likely to arise over the neighborhood's mandate and the extent of its authority. It is hard to achieve a clear separation of powers in any intergovernmental relationship, but it is especially hard to do so when the two "authorities" constantly interact in policymaking and administration. In any case, arguments over authority are inherently difficult to resolve. Where they rest on ambiguity or different interpretations, there is no recourse except to renegotiate the contract of decentralization. In general, these arguments over authority raise ultimate questions about the rules of the game that cannot be decided by recourse to those rules. Symbolically, community school board leaders complain that they feel like "lackeys" when they have to follow Board of Education directives and when they have to "check with downtown before we do anything." In this case, sharing authority means that neighborhood leaders are not fully their own masters and, in the view of some, they are still "under the thumbs" of the central government.

Conflict over responsibilities is also widespread in the closely "intertwined" experiments. Consider the New Haven Model Cities program. A conflict has existed there, since the experiment began, between the city agency and the neighborhood over the division of work responsibilities. The argument about "who should be doing what" has spilled over into other policymaking areas, thus, souring the entire relationship between the city and the neighborhood. In particular, neighborhood leaders complain that they have to do all the hard "street level" work, but they do not get any credit for their labors and lack authority commensurate with their responsibility. City administrations voice precisely the opposite complaint. They feel they are the only participants working effectively at the street level and resent the claim by neighborhood leaders that only they speak and work for the community.

Problems of communication exist in most organizations; and, in fact, it is hard enough for neighborhood leaders to coordinate the various parts of their own structure. However, the communications problem is compounded in "intertwined" experiments where two parallel bureaucracies overlap, interact, and conflict in the decisionmaking process. In the case of the neighborhood corporations, local leaders complain that they must spend an inordinate amount of time and energy meeting with their city counterparts to find out what is going on and to keep CPI (Community Progress, Inc.) from sneaking things past them.

In contrast, leaders of block associations and the Hill Health Corporation experience little friction with government because their experiments are relatively independent of government. This makes their decisionmaking less constrained and complicated; they do not have to look over their shoulders constantly to see what their partners in government are doing or planning.

The Costs of Political Controversy

A final structural variable concerns the nature of the political issues raised by different decentralization experiments. Some kinds of decentralization are inherently controversial, others not. When decentralization involves the governance of schools and attendant racial conflicts, political visibility is high and so are the perceived political consequences. Similarly, the Model Cities program inevitably raises controversial political issues: who gets what amount of program money and patronage jobs. In a third case, community boards exist to deal with the issues "everyone's upset about," as one member put it. And unless the community is unified in its sense of needs and interests, this means political controversy and conflict. In Community Board #3, for example, a bitter political conflict developed between low-income and middle-income residents over the housing policy for the neighborhoods. Low-income residents argued that only low-income housing should be built on the Lower East Side. Middle-income residents wanted middle-income as well as low-income housing built. The result was a stalemate and increased bitterness on both sides. In contrast, there is little political controversy in the delivery of health services (Hill Health Corporation) or in the delivery of other routine service problems (Community Task Force). Block associations also avoid political controversy by emphasizing common interests such as garbage collection, crime, and street lighting.

In sum, the more politically controversial the experiment, the less margin of error and flexibility the experiments will have in developing a program. Controversial experiments will be closely watched and quickly attacked by opponents. They are relatively defenseless against "smear" campaigns designed to discredit neighborhood democracy, and they run the risk of becoming "political footballs" in larger political arenas. All things being equal, the more controversial the experiment, the more difficult it will be to maintain political viability and to have an impact on neighborhood problems.

Political Skills and Resources

Faced with these tasks and organizational costs, leaders of the decentralization experiments apply whatever political skills and resources they possess to the challenge of making neighborhood government work. We have seen that the difficulty of the tasks and the magnitude of the costs differ greatly from experiment to experiment. But the skills and resources possessed by neighborhood leaders are surprisingly similar, and this similarity exists because all leaders lack several important resources.

Time Resources

For one thing, almost none of the leaders are paid for their work. This means that they must support their activism with private resources. None of the leaders could quit their regular jobs and still afford to be community activists. For this reason, no neighborhood leaders could afford to work full time. The leaders with the greatest time resources are self-employed small businessmen and employees of community organizations. The small businessmen often have a flexible schedule if their business permits them to set their own agenda. Employees of community organizations are paid to be neighborhood activists, and their job responsibilities often fit in naturally with other kinds of participation.

In general, the time resources of neighborhood leaders are limited and strictly bounded. Participation becomes a form of moonlighting, and the amount of time leaders can spend on neighborhood work depends on how many meetings they can endure each week and how many hours of sleep they require each night.

Expertise

Neighborhood leaders typically lack another important resource: administrative expertise.[8] Although most leaders do not have to run organizations on a day-to-day basis, most leaders must deal with problems of information gathering, analysis, budgeting, administrative process, implementation, and evaluation. Some leaders have learned these skills the hard way: for example, those ombudsmen who have learned "administrative process" in years of trying to work with city government. But most leaders of decentralization experiments readily admit that they lack necessary administrative skills. One school board member said:

> It is one thing to make a protest and tell the government what it's doing wrong when the problem is something you know about directly and run into every day. It's another thing to run things yourself . . . to figure out the budget and make decisions on time . . . and get through all the reports so you know what's going on and can see what's wrong in one program and know what to do about it.

This problem has affected participation in one successful experiment, the Hill Health Corporation. After a few meetings a majority of the newly elected consumer representatives stopped participating. Why? Because, according to one representative who stayed active, they "weren't prepared for the job. They didn't know what they were getting into. They didn't know how to deal with the technical stuff . . . the complicated medical talk . . . and they felt useless. So they stopped coming . . . You can't walk in off the street and run a big operation like this health center."

Staff Support

A third political resource that most neighborhood leaders lack is staff support. Some experiments, like the community school boards and the Hill Health Corporation, provide secretaries to organize the work of neighborhood participants. But no experiment provides neighborhood leaders with even minimal staff support to organize information and do research on current issues. Thus, the neighborhood leaders must absorb relevant information, analyze policies, and make decisions in their spare time. Any U.S. representative faced with this prospect would be completely ineffectual. And higher level representatives do not have to cope with the problem of shaping their role, making an initial impact, and keeping their institutions alive.

Fiscal Resources

Finally, neighborhood leaders lack flexible fiscal resources. And those that appear on paper to have substantial resources, such as the community school boards and the Model Cities program, lack flexible resources that can be used for new initiatives. As we have seen the community school boards have only Title I funds to "play around with," and the resources in Model Cities are largely divided between city departments and existing neighborhood organizations.

Armed with these meager political resources, leaders of the decentralization experiments must rely on their exuberance, street level experience, and their "mother-wit" as one leader put it. But in the hard accounting of political costs and resources, these are relatively intangible weapons. We may admire the personal qualities of neighborhood leaders, but administration is not power. In short, neighborhood leaders lack the resources to convert investment into impact in the face of difficult tasks and high political and organizational costs.

The Political Economy of Neighborhood Experiments

The idea of political economy, as it is used here, concerns the tasks, costs, and resources found in different decentralization structures.[9] My argument is simply that neighborhood structures will be effective only if their resources are commensurate with their tasks and costs. Only under this condition will investments in decentralization be converted into impacts. We have seen that the resources possessed by neighborhood leaders are similar. We have also seen that the tasks and costs of decentralization vary dramatically. The crucial variables are as follows:

	A. Task Orientation
1. Focused	Diffuse
2. Flexible	Inflexible
3. Simple	Complex
	B. Organizational Costs
4. Informal	Formal
5. Small-Scale	Neighborhoodwide
6. Small Group	Large Assembly
7. Autonomy	Intertwined (dependent)
	C. Political Costs
8. Noncontroversial	Controversial

The more the decentralization experiments possess characteristics in the right-hand column, the harder it will be for them to have an impact on neighborhood problems. No single characteristic totally vitiates the possibility of success in decentralization. But, in fact, the characteristics are strongly related. Three experiments, the community boards, Model Cities, and the community school boards are diffuse, complex, and formal. They also have large governing bodies, are closely intertwined with government, and raise controversial political issues. A fourth experiment, neighborhood corporations, is similar in most respects. Three other experiments, block associations, the Community Task Force, and the Hill Health Corporation have the opposite characteristics in almost every respect. Analytically, we would predict that the first set of experiments would have little impact on neighborhood problems because of the tasks and costs that they face and that the second set of experiments would far more easily have an impact on their neighborhoods. This prediction is borne out by both the evidence on initiatives and impacts and by the evidence on the neighborhood leaders' sense of political efficacy.

Two Approaches to Decentralization

Most plans for decentralization strive for formal neighborhood democracy and entail the creation of neighborhoodwide assemblies with broad mandates.

Indeed, prior national policy as expressed in community corporations and Model Cities points in that direction. Recent plans for decentralization in New York, Minneapolis, and Boston also follow the model of formal, comprehensive neighborhood democracy.[10]

We have seen that this structural model involves inherently difficult tasks and imposes high political and organizational costs. Alternatives to this model exist in block associations, the Community Task Force, the Hill Health Corporation and in certain kinds of neighborhood corporations. In theory, despite the major differences in task and cost, the choice between the formal, comprehensive model of neighborhood democracy and its alternatives is a real one. The choice depends on the amount of resources that government and society wish to allocate to neighborhood institutions. It depends too on the amount of risk society wants to take with decentralization. In a diving competition, the probability of doing well on an easy dive is relatively high, but the maximum score is limited. The diver gets less points for an easy dive. The total score is a function of the degree of difficulty and skill in execution (variables that tend to vary inversely). Decentralization experiments are similar. The experiments that attack relatively simple problems of service delivery have a good chance to fulfill their objectives. But these experiments do not have the breadth to attack or solve more difficult neighborhood problems. By contrast, neighborhood democracy in its formal comprehensive form seeks to perform the most difficult tasks, and the likelihood of success is low. But if formal neighborhood institutions possessed sufficient resources and skills to convert investment into impact on the difficult problems, the overall impact of decentralization might be far greater.

8 Making Decentralization Work: The View from City Hall

Up to this point, we have explained the impacts of decentralization experiments solely in terms of the political economy of neighborhood organization. But this explanation is incomplete in one important respect: it overlooks the role of city hall in the process of decentralization. Although many neighborhood leaders like to think they work alone, city hall plays an active role in most decentralization experiments.[1] And although many neighborhood leaders view city hall as a foe of decentralization, some city halls have tried to take the lead in "making decentralization work."

In both New York and New Haven, decentralization experiments have been launched or aided by central government. But only in New York has city hall consciously forged and tested a variety of decentralization strategies. It was New York that experienced the searing crisis over school decentralization. And it is New York that has a central Office of Neighborhood Government, Community Cabinets in several neighborhoods, and a great number of street-level government offices. Because New York has had the richest experience with decentralization, it has also had the most extensive education in the problems of making decentralization work. Although it is simplistic and perhaps misguided to draw general "lessons" from the New York experience, it is possible to see clearly in this setting how city hall approaches the problem of decentralization and what obstacles to decentralization exist within central government.

The Evolution of City Hall Initiatives

In 1960, no city government knew how to decentralize. As we have seen, decentralization had little intellectual support and even less precedent (until very recently) in urban government. "Community action" was a shot in the dark, and the initiatives that followed community action were no less experimental and uncertain. In New York the impetus to decentralization grew out of a strong determination to prevent riots during the "long hot summers" of the late 1960s. Mayor Lindsay dramatized his concern by touring the streets of poor neighborhoods. At the same time, city hall aides, working behind the scenes, established a network of contacts with neighborhood leaders. The idea was to keep city hall in touch with "what was happening on the streets" and thus to defuse highly charged conflicts before they exploded into riots. This early monitoring effort constituted decentralization in its weakest form: information gathering and consultation with neighborhood residents. However, as the communications network developed, the relationship between city hall and the neighborhoods gradually changed. Neighborhood leaders began to channel local complaints and requests to their city hall "contacts." At the same time, city hall aides began to dispense what one called "minor league patronage–bus rides, baseball tickets, free movies"–to their new neighborhood constituencies. The result was that, almost by accident, city hall developed an informal ombudsman mechanism operating outside of existing government structures. This mechanism, when institutionalized, became the Mayor's Urban Action Task Force.[2]

The evolution of the Mayor's Task Force provides several important insights into the process of decentralization. First, since no one knows how to decentralize government, the process is hard to predict: initiatives will evolve in unexpected ways, and the result, where successful, will rely as much on serendipity as on far-sighted planning. Further, however the process develops, city hall must contribute three ingredients: flexibility, access, and visible benefits. The first ingredient permits central government to stay in the "game" as it changes, the second enables city hall and the neighborhoods to work out new rules of the game, and the third makes the game worth playing for neighborhood residents. Importantly, it was not the symbolism of the mayor's walking tours alone that enabled the Task Force to mobilize neighborhood resources. It was also the fact that riots did not break out and that the task force responded to neighborhood complaints and requests. The task force was successful in its limited operations precisely because it was not a symbolic initiative: it produced tangible results for those neighborhood leaders who helped the mayor keep his city "cool."

The Political Costs of Decentralization

In 1969, New York initiated political decentralization with three experiments in "community control" of schools. These experiments, widely reported because of the crisis in Ocean Hill-Brownsville, proved a costly political lesson for the Lindsay administration. If nothing else, the experiments showed that decentralization, when undertaken haphazardly, can arouse the bitterest conflicts in urban politics: black against white, neighborhood against public employees, neighborhood against city hall, city hall against union, and city hall against independent agency (Board of Education). Various writers have tried to explain why the Ocean Hill-Brownsville experiment failed so dramatically.[3] Those who have examined the fiasco pin the blame on different villains, but this scapegoating misses the point. For in a climate of racial conflict, a formal neighborhoodwide experiment that dealt with an intractable urban problem, that was closely and confusingly entangled with city government, that was politically controversial, and that lacked resources, had enough costs and conflicts built into its basic structure to guarantee failure. The Lindsay administration's reaction to the "crisis in the schools" was to pull back from decentralization strategies that involved citizen participation and community control. City hall turned instead to the idea of administrative decentralization in designing new plans and initiatives.[4] According to one city hall aide:

> The Ocean Hill mess almost killed us politically. It was a no-win policy . . . You can't expect us to make the same mistake all over again . . . If I went to the mayor with another plan for community control, I'd be looking for a new job tomorrow.

Clearly, decentralization carries high political costs for city hall as well as for the neighborhoods. Decentralization is most attractive as an alternative to existing urban policy before it has been tried—when it offers the plausible hope that if centralization does not work, the structural opposite will. But as soon as decentralization is implemented, city hall faces a stringent political economy of its own. If decentralization required no investment of political resources by city hall, mayors might experiment widely with different strategies. But when decentralization generates severe political conflict, city hall will look to see what results it is getting for the added political costs it is forced to bear. This calculation is easily made in the case of Ocean Hill-Brownsville. The same calculation was made by former Mayor Lee of New Haven, who decided that the only sensible way to deal with the Model Cities program was to stay as far away from it as possible.[5] In general, because citizens have high expectations of decentralization and because it is an unknown quantity, city hall officials must make their strategy work quickly and visibly. In this respect, the political economy of decentralization is the same in city hall as it is in the neighborhoods.

The Impact of Street-level Offices

In New York and elsewhere, city hall has pursued administrative decentralization by creating street-level offices in its own image.[6] In fact, in many cities, these offices are called "little city halls." The logic of this strategy is deceptively simple. If city hall is too big and too distant, why not retail the product and give neighborhoods their own piece of government? According to this logic, an official sitting in city hall would simply identify his neighborhoods, figure out where to place a little city hall in each one, and thus produce a proximate, accessible system of "neighborhood government." The actual result is likely to differ sharply from this blueprint, however, and in what follows we will show the limits of street-level governments (constructed on the little city hall model) and will also examine several obstacles to decentralization within city government.

In judging the impact of street-level offices, we must have some idea of what they are designed to produce. Is the goal greater government presence and proximity, a referral service, or the successful clearance of complaints? Obviously, the requirements for efficiency differ widely with different goals. If government simply seeks a presence, small kiosks with a city employee on duty at all times might suffice. If the goal is the successful clearance of complaints, the street-level offices require far greater capabilities. In what follows we assume that, at a minimum, street-level offices are supposed to be effective complaint-gathering centers and that this function presumes both government presence and proximity. The logic of service delivery is clear here. If field offices are to be successful in complaint gathering, it is necessary that they be visible to and well known by neighborhood residents and that they be conveniently located.[7] My argument is that street-level offices often have trouble meeting even these simple tests.

If storefronts are intended to "personalize" government by putting an arm of city hall within easy walking distance, we need to analyze what counts as "easy access." Clearly, a neighborhood office serving Manhattan, but located on Times Square would have little meaning for the residents of Harlem or the Lower East Side. The question is: how close to a citizen does a storefront have to be to fulfill the criterion of proximity?

Below we will offer a crude picture of what is involved in the notion of easy "walking distance." The analysis, based on observed pedestrian movement on the Lower East Side, tried to determine how long it took different pedestrians to walk one north-south block and one east-west block.[8] On north-south blocks, the fastest walkers could cover a single block in 45 seconds, the slowest in a minute and a half. On the longer east-west blocks, the fastest walkers managed a block in just over two minutes, the slowest in three minutes. The average travel time for north-south blocks was one minute, for east-west blocks, two and one-half minutes. The implication of this analysis should be clear. If one sets a five-minute walk as the outer limit of easy walking distance, storefronts will only cover five blocks in a north or south direction and two blocks east or west. If one sets the limit at ten minutes, coverage will be ten blocks north or south, four blocks east or west. Of course, "easy access" is increased if one takes public transportation or a car, but this also creates costs in money and convenience—and there may be a considerable walking distance left if public transit is indirect, as it is likely to be. The point is simply that it is hard to create easy interaction between citizens and government offices unless scores of street-level offices are created throughout the neighborhood.

"Coverage": Empirical Tests

By creating a crude model of easy walking distance, we have indicated the limited coverage of street-level bureau offices. A more direct way to analyze the impact of street-level government is to ask residents of a neighborhood if they know about street-level offices. This test was made by asking 100 Lower East Side residents if they knew where to find the local office of the Mayor's Task Force. To test the hypothesis that more people would know about government storefronts the closer one is to the office, the first fifty interviews were conducted within a three-block radius of the office. In that area, only three of the fifty residents knew that a task force existed and where it was located. Six people questioned on the block where the office was located were unaware of its existence. Eight other residents gave directions to other local community organizations.

Fifty more residents were interviewed in an area within six blocks of the task force office, but outside the three block radius. Of this group, only one resident knew about the task force, but had no idea where it was. Other residents pointed out community organizations, housing projects, social clubs, and even the police station. One Puerto Rican woman was sure the office had burned down the past week. It had not. Finally, we asked three policemen on foot patrol in the neighborhood if they knew the task force office and if so, where it was located. None did.[9] In sum, the evidence of these informal interviews clearly shows that the task force offices are invisible in the neighborhood they seek to serve—at least on the Lower East Side.

This finding is confirmed by a survey of 450 residents in three neighborhoods. In the survey, citizens were asked if they knew about different neighborhood offices in their immediate area.[10] In Washington Heights, residents were asked about the community school board, the Washington Heights Health Center, and the Neighborhood Action Plan office (an office concerned with planning and housing maintenance). In Crown Heights, citizens were asked about their Neighborhood Action Plan office, community school board, community corporation, and neighborhood multiservice center. In Bushwick, citizens were asked about their community school board, community corporation job center, Urban Action Task Force office, and public health care center. The findings given in Table 8-1 show that the recognition rate was under 33 percent in ten of the twelve cases. Only the two health services achieved high recognition rates: 58 percent in the case of the Washington Heights health center and 68 percent in the case of the Bushwick public health care center. Significantly, only these two street-level offices provided tangible services to neighborhood residents. The negative implication is that not only do the more comprehensive experiments fail to make a substantial impact on neighborhood problems, but they also have shallow roots in the community.

The "City Hall" Model and its Deficiencies

To the extent that neighborhood institutions are built on the model of city hall, as governments-in-miniature, their impact is likely to be severely limited. On the one hand, if city hall tries to create formal neighborhood assemblies in its own

Table 8-1
Citizen Recognition of Street-level Government Offices

Washington Heights		
Neighborhood Action Program	21%	(31)
Community School Board	33%	(50)
Washington Heights Health Center	58%	(88)
		(N=150)
Crown Heights		
Neighborhood Action Program	13%	(20)
Crown Heights Community Corporation	21%	(31)
Neighborhood Multiservice Center	31%	(47)
Community School Board	23%	(35)
		(N=150)
Bushwick		
Bushwick Community Corporation	26%	(38)
Job Center	24%	(35)
Task Force Office	11%	(16)
Public Health Care Center	68%	(102)
Community School Board	27%	(40)
		(N=150)

image (i.e., little city councils), it is likely to produce experiments lacking sufficient resources to meet their tasks and organizational costs. On the other hand, if city hall tries to create street-level offices in its own image (i.e., little city halls), it is likely to produce institutions that have shallow roots and limited coverage. Significantly, the strengths and weaknesses of the two models are complementary. The former needs greater administrative power and expertise, the latter requires greater citizen participation. In theory, the road to "comprehensive" decentralization would therefore appear to lie in a synthesis of the two models. In practice, however, if it is difficult to establish either the political or the administrative model, it is likely to be at least twice as difficult to create a synthesis of the two, because there are existing obstacles to comprehensive decentralization at the neighborhood level and within city government. We have already examined the obstacles at the neighborhood level. We now turn to an examination of obstacles to decentralization within city government.

Obstacles to Decentralization Within City Government

The success of decentralization also depends on the ability of city hall to coordinate its policies and services and on the ability of street-level bureaucrats to work directly with neighborhood leaders. In New York, these conditions of decentralization did not exist, and bringing them about became city hall's chief task in trying to make decentralization work. For if neighborhood leaders confront a fragmented central government, they will have great difficulty in putting together coherent policies and services at the local level. And if street-level bureaucrats lack the flexibility and authority to tailor services to neighborhood needs, neighborhood government becomes, according to one leader, a "cart without a horse." In short, if city hall wants decentralization to work, it must coordinate its services and also force decisionmaking power downward in the administrative system. The mayor's executive assistant for neighborhood government put the problem this way:

Our experience has taught us that there must be local officers with sufficient authority to make a difference in the delivery of city services *before* the residents of an area either will want to or will be able to participate effectively.

And further:

The city's practice over the last years, both in administrative reform and in citizen participation, has been to allow each administrator to proceed along his own path at his own pace. This has led to increased fragmentation (and frustration) of citizen involvement . . . at the local level and to what some observers have called a system of 'functional feudalism'.[11]

The Problem of Coordination

Coordination is not a new problem in urban government. It is an effect of the structural fragmentation that has characterized the urban political system since the early nineteenth century. As we have seen, the bosses used the machine as an instrument of coordination, progressive reformers used the council-manager form of government and the professional bureaucracy, and later reformers looked to the strong mayor charter as a way of consolidating and coordinating governmental power. In New York in the late 1960s, the Lindsay administration initiated another coordinating device: the reorganization of existing departments into highly centralized superagencies. But even increased centralization did not solve the problem of coordination. And when city hall moved toward decentralization, the utility of the superagencies became even more doubtful. According to one city hall official:

The superagencies have had little impact on the coordination of local, operational responsibilities. While the Mayor may have reduced the number of people he has to deal with to get a decision, this reorganization has made little difference to communities seeking help. They still have to deal with 50 separate departments. If anything, the system is sometimes less efficient for them because the administration superstructure added additional levels of decisionmaking at the top without securing comparable coordination at the community level.[12]

Meanwhile, the familiar coordination problems remain. According to city hall's own analysis, little communication exists between administrations, and agencies within the same administration have only tenuous working relationships.[13] More important, if central control is weak, so is the authority and flexibility of neighborhood-level officials. Some administrations have no district-level officials at all, and those that do find that bureau chiefs and agency heads resist any movement to decentralize bureaucratic power.

The Problem of Cooperation

The role of neighborhood public employees is central to any decentralization experiment. It is the teachers, policemen, firemen, and garbagemen who deliver public services at the point of contact with citizens and who must work directly with neighborhood leaders in the day-to-day administration of decentralized government. It is these employees, too, who are often criticized harshly by neighborhood residents and reformers alike for "insensitivity," "incompetence," and for "resisting change." Whatever the validity of these charges, it is clear that street-level bureaucrats and neighborhood leaders must cooperate with one another if decentralization is to work.

To find out how street-level bureaucrats view their jobs, their problems, and the issue of decentralization, we interviewed sixty public employees in four neighborhoods of New York.[14] The city employees were foremen, supervisors, and uniformed officers in the police, sanitation, traffic, highways, parks, health services, addiction services, housing, and city planning departments. Although different public employees have different problems and agendas, the interviews revealed several common patterns. Significantly, these patterns have important implications for the ability of street-level bureaucrats to cooperate with neighborhood leaders and residents in the process of decentralization. First, street-level bureaucrats rarely work with their counterparts in other services. The lack of service coordination that exists at the top of city government extends down to the street level. Second, only a small percentage of street-level bureaucrats said that they had either "fairly much" or "very much" say in "what is planned by your agency for your district." Rather, the vast majority of neighborhood public employees felt that they "need to have more say" in planning and policymaking in their agencies. Their main problems, as they see it, are that they lack adequate information about what their agency and other agencies are doing, and they also lack the flexibility and authority required to do their job. Third, in working with the community, the neighborhood public employees feel that they lack channels of communication with neighborhood residents, are often asked to deal with problems outside of their jurisdiction, and are unable to reach agreement about mutual responsibilities with neighborhood leaders and other agencies. Finally, street-level bureaucrats repeatedly express two basic attitudes toward decentralization. First, they seek greater autonomy and thus support any impetus to administrative decentralization. Second, most believe that increased citizen involvement would increase "cooperation" and that greater cooperation would mitigate their problems of communication and coordination.

Two Obstacles to Administrative Decentralization

Two apparent contradictions exist in a strategy that attempts to make city government more responsive and its policies more coherent through administrative decentralization. Most important, if fragmentation in government undermines coordination, it seems contradictory to seek greater coordination through a strategy of decentralization that inevitably fragments decisionmaking even further. Second, we know that street-level bureaucrats already possess unusual discretion and clear responsibility in delivering services. If neighborhood residents decry existing service delivery, it seems contradictory to give increased power and authority to those who have failed in the first place.

In light of these apparent contradictions, two sorts of arguments can be made for decentralization. The first argument is essentially negative and suggests that alternatives to a neighborhood approach are unpromising at best. For one thing, the experience in New York shows the difficulty of coordinating a large city government at the city hall level. Further, it is virtually impossible to control street-level bureaucrats from city hall, given the discretion inherent in the role of teachers, policemen, firemen, and the rest.[15] The positive argument is based on the premise that decentralization will actually resolve the apparent contradictions discussed above. For one thing, the organizational costs of coordinating a large government at the center are prohibitive—and the attempt to do so leads only to new layers of coordinating committees, the solution may be to coordinate the work of low-level employees at the point of direct contact with citizens. That is, the alternative to restructuring the entire government so as to coordinate service delivery is simply to coordinate those street-level bureaucrats who personally deliver services. This strategy also requires a greater devolution of authority to neighborhood administrators and thus speaks to the second apparent contradiction of administrative decentralization. For even though street-level bureaucrats have discretion and responsibility in service delivery, they typically lack the authority to make changes responsive to neighborhood needs. Although discretion may be a necessary condition of responsive administration, flexibility and authority are also necessary conditions. As one street-level bureaucrat put it, "the way it is now, we catch all the flack, but we don't have the power to put things right . . . You get tired of being the villain when your hands are tied.

This analysis of administrative decentralization finds empirical support in the recent New York experiments with community service cabinets. The idea of the cabinets is straightforward: "to place the power and responsibility for local decisions with the district offices of each agency who work in the communities they serve," and to "establish a local cabinet of these officers to integrate the planning and operations of the multiple city services in each of these areas."[16] Although it is too early to make a confident assessment of the impact of the community cabinets, the early experience gives a clear indication of when the cabinets would work and when they would not. Minutes of cabinet meetings show that when the neighborhood cabinet members raised general problems of coordination and service delivery, they functioned much like community boards, with "lots of talk and little action." In contrast, when the agency representatives focused on concrete service problems that required their cooperation, decisions were made and quick actions resulted. This experience has led the newly appointed district managers who coordinate the work of the cabinet to search for "winning issues": those problems that can be solved "tomorrow" and whose solution would give street-level bureaucrats a sense of confidence and accomplishment. The implication of this experience is that coordination and cooperation, so hard to produce at the city hall level, can be achieved by small units dealing with concrete problems at the point of impact on the neighborhood. Again, the political economy of decentralization appears to be the same for street-level bureaucrats as it is for neighborhood leaders.

Conclusion: Decentralization as a Learning Process

City hall aides in the Office of Neighborhood Government believe that any attempt to decentralize city government involves a long-term learning process. They began, as one put it, "with a very crude idea of what neighborhood was where, what local administrators did, and what local services looked like . . . basically we didn't know a hell of a lot about anything." In trying to make decentralization work, city hall aides also learned some concrete lessons. They learned that strategies that work in one neighborhood will not always work in another. For this reason, they believe that decentralization initiatives cannot be uniform and universal. Rather, as one city hall aide put it, designs for decentralization must follow "the lay of the land"; or in the more vivid words of a neighborhood leader, "it's a matter of different strokes for different folks."

City hall aides have also found that any central government initiative will cause deep mistrust in some if not most segments of the neighborhood. One New

York aide has worked for two years to convince groups in one neighborhood that administrative decentralization is not "a political takeover" by the mayor. But given the diversity and intricacy of neighborhood organization, any such attempt to bring city hall and the neighborhoods together on a common venture in decentralization is bound to take a long time. If decentralization is a learning process for city hall, it is also one for street-level bureaucrats and neighborhood leaders. Not only does city hall have to learn about the neighborhood, but neighborhood leaders and street-level bureaucrats also have to learn about each other; and street-level bureaucrats have to learn how to work with their counterparts in other agencies. If decentralization is thus a learning process for all concerned, how is the requisite education achieved? The answer that emerges from the evidence presented above is that the learning process works best when all participants—street-level bureaucrats and neighborhood leaders alike—are involved in concrete initiatives in neighborhood problem-solving initiatives designed to achieve tangible results.

9 The Future of Neighborhood Government: Consensus and Conflict

Why are there not more decentralization experiments in American cities? After all, it is apparent that many citizens, community leaders, and government officials favor the policy. The argument of this chapter is that although the idea of neighborhood government receives broad support, specific plans for neighborhood government arouse intense opposition.

A survey of 450 citizens in three neighborhoods of New York City revealed strong support for the idea of neighborhood government.[1] In Washington Heights, a racially mixed neighborhood in Manhattan, 73 percent of those interviewed said they favored the idea. In Crown Heights, a mixed neighborhood in Brooklyn, 73 percent also expressed their support (see Table 9-1). A majority of every ethnic group favored neighborhood government as did a majority in every age group and every sector of the neighborhood. In Washington Heights, for example, 89 percent of black residents favored neighborhood government as did 85 percent of Puerto Rican residents, 68 percent of Catholic residents, and 60 percent of Jewish residents. Some variation in support was found in different subneighborhoods. There was nearly unanimous support in one section containing old housing and a predominance of minority group members; and 62 percent support in one section having an older white population.[a]

Residents in the three neighborhoods were also asked why they favored or opposed neighborhood government. The leading responses were that citizens believed neighborhood government would make government more responsive and stimulate cooperation among local residents. Among those who opposed the concept, the reasons given most frequently were that neighborhood government would fragment city government and create unwanted burdens and involvements for local residents. As Table 9-2 shows, 27.2 percent of the respondents in Washington Heights said that neighborhood government would stimulate local cooperation, while 24 percent believed that neighborhood government would produce greater responsiveness. Another 12 percent viewed neighborhood government as a way to tap local expertise. A smaller percentage thought that neighborhood government would give neighborhood people more power and "say" in government.

Among the community leaders involved in decentralization experiments in

[a]In general, opposition to neighborhood government increased with age and length of residence in the area. These variables largely coincide with ethnicity, and the inference can be drawn in Washington Heights (and in the other neighborhoods) that the older, white population is less eager to experiment with neighborhood government.

Table 9-1
Support for Neighborhood Government in Three Neighborhoods

Question: Do you favor neighborhood government?

	Washington Heights	Crown Heights	Bushwick
Yes	73% (110)	73% (110)	81% (121)
No	20% (30)	16% (24)	13% (19)
Don't Know	4% (6)	6% (9)	5% (8)
No Answer	3% (5)	5% (7)	1% (2)
	N=150	N=150	N=150

Table 9-2
Perceptions of Neighborhood Government (by neighborhood)

Question: Why do you favor or oppose neighborhood government?

	Washington Heights	Crown Heights	Bushwick
For:			
Responsiveness	24% (36)	29% (43)	30% (45)
More Say	6% (9)	5% (7)	2% (3)
Local Expertise	12% (18)	5% (8)	18% (27)
Local Cooperation	27% (41)	25% (37)	17% (26)
Local Priorities	7% (10)	7% (10)	11% (16)
Against:			
Corruption	3% (5)	1% (1)	1% (2)
Fragmentation	1% (2)	3% (4)	5% (7)
Against Involvement	5% (7)	13% (20)	2% (3)
Taxes, Burdens	2% (3)	3% (4)	7% (10)
Don't Know	13% (19)	11% (16)	7% (11)
	100%	100% (150)	100% (150)

New York and New Haven, support for increased neighborhood government was unanimous. However, neighborhood leaders expressed diverse images of what kind of neighborhood government should be implemented. Some wanted a self-sufficient, tax-raising neighborhood government "like the suburbs have,"[2] as one leader put it. Others simply wanted to strengthen existing experiments through increased resources and opposed giving neighborhoods either taxing power or the power to hire and fire public employees.

At the same time, most neighborhood leaders agreed about why decentralization should be pursued. Like the citizens interviewed, neighborhood leaders believed that decentralized government would foster responsiveness and cooperation and, in particular, would take advantage of neighborhood skills and expertise. As one leader put it, "we know what's going on out here; we know what this community needs; and we know how to get things done with neighborhood folks. The people in city hall don't have a clue." Similarly, in the words of one neighborhood corporation leader in New Haven, "I don't know who got the idea that there's only a handful of people who should be allowed to govern themselves and the rest of us. From what I've seen there's a lot of talent out here on the streets, and that's what we're trying to prove in the corporation."

Most of the neighborhood public employees interviewed in New York also supported the idea of neighborhood government.[3] But the idea was perceived by public employees in terms of administrative decentralization: devolving more power and discretion to district officials. To the public employees, there was a great difference between gaining more power themselves and giving power to neighborhood residents. As one sanitation foreman put it, "It comes down to who's telling us to do what. What good does it do us if you take power from the commissioners and give it to the community. We're taking orders either way."

Finally, city officials involved in decentralization experiments expressed cautious support for neighborhood government. Again, images differed. Some city hall administrators expressed a commitment in principle to community control. But the majority favored a gradual evolution toward greater decentralization, and most preferred a strategy of administrative decentralization. One said, "You can't do this kind of thing overnight. If it doesn't work, we get the heat. So I suppose we want to keep a pretty firm hand on the reins." A small percentage of these city hall administrators felt that decentralization should be "stopped cold." "I've been burned once, and it won't happen again," said one. "We're supposed to be decentralizing," said another. "But like the man said, watch what we do, not what we say."

These surveys reveal broad support for the idea of neighborhood government. But reactions to specific plans for neighborhood government were highly critical, full of deep-seated conflicts. If one assumes that neighborhood government can work only if neighborhoods want it (and it seems contradictory to force neighborhood leaders to participate in a decentralization experiment they oppose), conflicts over specific plans severely diminish the political viability of decentralization.

These patterns of consensus and conflict appear in citizen responses to a *Plan for Neighborhood Government* presented by the mayor of New York in 1970. After announcing the plan, the mayor held a series of consultations over a two-month period with neighborhood officials and community groups. According to the mayor's report on these consultations:

> 200 local meetings took place, and representatives of over 3,000 citywide and community organizations participated in (the) consultations. While some meetings had several hundred people in attendance, most meetings were kept much smaller, generally with no more than 20 people invited to participate. Beyond these formal consultation meetings, we (the mayor's office) received several hundred detailed written commentaries on the *Plan for Neighborhood Government* from civic associations. Community Planning Boards, Community Corporations, fraternal organizations, block associations, elected officials, union representatives, academicians, and students.[4]

The mayor proposed that existing neighborhood agencies be consolidated into a "comprehensive neighborhood government system." The plan would establish a single "Community Board . . . with full-time staff, community offices, and a Community Cabinet of local city officials." The goal was to "provide one local body to deal with all city problems, with a broadly based membership and the capacity to monitor effectively local services" which would "end duplication, broaden citizen involvement in governmental decisionmaking and make city agencies more accountable to the communities they serve."[5]

The community boards would have a minimum of twenty-four members, appointed at first in a "tripartite appointment process" by the mayor, the borough president, and city councilmen. Moreoever, "formal membership on the Community Boards would be extended to representatives from the Community School Boards" and where appropriate, the Anti-Poverty Community Corporations and the Model Cities Advisory Committees."[b]

The plan clearly was not designed to bring about immediate community control, and some neighborhood leaders opposed it for this reason. In general, although the consultations revealed almost universal support for the idea of neighborhood government, more than 75 percent of the neighborhood organizations and individuals "consulted" opposed the mayor's plan. A content analysis of consultation minutes and letters from citizens and community groups shows

[b]At a later date, according to the mayor's plan, community board representatives would be elected by neighborhood residents–on a "Community Election Day." In addition, the mayor would appoint a community director "from a panel of five names submitted by the Community Board." The boards would possess the powers presently held by existing neighborhood organizations including advisory planning, ombudsman-style grievance articulation, and the administration of certain neighborhood programs. Further, the new community boards would receive the necessary information and power to monitor and evaluate city services.

more than twenty recurrent themes in citizen objections to the plan.[6] As Table 9-3 indicates, more than ten "themes" were strongly emphasized, demonstrating the diversity of citizen objections. A second characteristic of citizen response was that many objections were in direct conflict. For example, one objection to the mayor's plan was that community boards were not given enough power (#2). But another objection was directly contradictory. Those who wanted to "strengthen existing units" (#4) felt that power should be given not to new community boards but to existing neighborhood institutions.

Further, although many participants in the consultations felt that the plan would produce greater governmental "coordination" (#10), many other participants felt the boards would be "just another committee" and that neighbor-

Table 9-3
Citizen Responses to Neighborhood Government Plan

Theme	Score
1. Election Procedures	122
2. Not Enough Power	98
3. Keep Politics (Mayor) Out	96
4. Strengthen Existing Units	85
5. Just Another Committee	72
6. Will Cost Too Much	68
7. Need More Money for Boards	66
8. Disagree with Neighborhood Boundaries	58
9. Good to Standardize Boundaries	52
10. Coordination Is Good	50
11. Need Better Service	45
12. Give Power to Borough Presidents	43
13. Will Cause Fragmentation	40
14. Not Enough Citizen Participation	40
15. Won't Solve Anything	38
16. Too Confusing	34
17. Need to Decentralize Departments	26
18. Residency Requirements	25
19. Boards Too Large	20
20. Need to Control Departments	18
21. Boards Too Small	18
22. Mechanisms Already Work	18
23. Training for Local Leaders	16
24. Will Take Too Long	13
25. Patronage and Corruption	12
26. Will Cause Conflict	6
27. Wrong Priorities	6

hoods already have too many committees (#5). Still others felt that if the community boards did not have general authority, they would simply "fragment" street-level government (#13).

Other conflicts between the major objections include the following:

1. Many neighborhood residents felt that not enough money was allocated to the neighborhoods (#7). But just as many objected that the plan would be too costly (#6).
2. One of city hall's leading arguments in favor of the plan was that it would standardize district boundaries used by police, sanitation, and other services. This view was also articulated by some participants in the consultation (#9). But an equal number of residents objected to the plan on the grounds that neighborhood boundaries were badly drawn (#8).
3. Some participants felt that decentralization could not work unless neighborhoods "controlled the departments" (#20). But a slightly larger number felt that district officials must be given more power and independence before decentralization could have any effect on service delivery (#17).
4. A small number of participants objected that the size of the community board was too large (#19) and would be "unwieldy"; but a similar number of participants felt the board was too small (#21) and hence exclusive.

Several other themes reveal the intrinsic difficulty of trying to launch a decentralization experiment. A number of participants felt the plan was "too confusing" (#16). Other neighborhood residents said that when city government proves it will spend money on services and deliver services more effectively (#11) then they will be willing to talk about "fancy ideas" like neighborhood government. Impatience was a factor in other objections in that some residents felt that it would "take too long" to get any results (#24).

These objections may come naturally to citizens who feel government is unresponsive and uncaring, but there is another objection that is more surprising. A central theme in the consultation was that neighborhood government should be free of politics—that "serving the community" means "keeping politics out" (#3). This antipolitical feeling was expressed in two ways. First, residents feared that the neighborhood government plan was merely a device to extend the mayor's power and to interfere politically in neighborhood affairs. According to one community board member, "This seems to be an attempt to achieve decentralization by extreme centralization. To put it more strongly, this seems to have the purpose of creating more patronage appointments for the mayor." Or, as one civic association president put it, "This is a political move, which we fully realize is the name of the game and which politicians must play to stay alive and in the forefront. But we don't want any part of city hall political games." Or again: "The plan is the antithesis of bringing government closer to the people. It would make appointments largely political." What this means, according to another community board member, is that "my planning board would vote it down simply on the basis that it was prepared by the mayor's office."

The second aspect of the "keep politics out" theme was the fear that neighborhood government would bring with it political hacks, porkbarrel, and selfish political conflict. According to one participant, "By introducing money the plan would turn the board into a big political thing instead of the bastion of volunteerism that neighborhood organization is today." In the view of a neighborhood minister, "The plan will bring out the political hacks of the community. The truly civic-minded would not be selected and they'll stay away to avoid the political wrangling."

Two further comments underscore the point:

> Instead of being a unifying force, this plan would serve to set one neighborhood against another and increase the bickering and division between groups in the neighborhood.
>
> The mayor, it would seem, would rather have neighborhood government become yet another arena for political conflict.

The effect of this antipolitical attitude was to arouse community resistance to political innovation. However, this strongly felt attitude was directly contradicted by another widespread attitude: that the plan was not political enough, that not enough political power was given to community residents (#2). This theme was expressed in the statement of a neighborhood organization in Brooklyn.

> We believe that this plan merely scratches the surface of democratic local government. Lacking are three elements essential to any realistic plan: (1) Democracy; (2) Authority; (3) Money. In order to achieve *democracy* local elections should replace planned appointments . . . We know it is difficult to get people to turn out for district elections, but this depends largely on *authority*. If there is authority in local office—if this is where the sanitation, police, fire, and other officials recognize as authority—if this is where local *decisions* are really made, people will know it—and vote. This authority depends on the adequate provision of *money*. We believe that neighborhood government must have the money to deliver services if it is to be any kind of government worth the name.

And, according to another civic association leader:

> The people must be given a chance to bring about a change in our government. But (the) plan does not give neighborhoods any real meaningful power to nail down irresponsible city agencies to perform their duties in order for the communities to benefit from them. I'm under the impression the plan is merely another falsehood.

Two further comments:

Unless full control is acceded to the local communities the term "neighborhood government" is meaningless.

No decisionmaking power. No budget . . . No accountability to the neighborhood . . . Do not give the illusion this has power.

These objections caused residents to question whether neighborhood government would solve any important problems (#15). According to one community organizer, "what shall happen is in two or three years we shall have another plan for community control that will replace this one just as this one seeks to replace these functioning agencies." And further:

If this plan is put into effect, there will be no perceptible improvement in the function of government. Nothing will change with crime or slum housing. People's frustration will be staggering"—(Queens Block Association president)

If these reactions are representative, the burden of proof placed on any neighborhood government experiment is great. It must be nonpolitical at the same time that it brings "real political power" to the neighborhoods. It must have an immediate, visible effect on major problems at the same time that delicate mechanisms for "neighborhood democracy" are established. Moreover, the local resident wants city hall to take strong initiatives that will improve neighborhood conditions at the same time that he strongly resents and resists central government interference.

Two Substantive Issues

Two issues lie at the heart of resistance to the plan for neighborhood government. The first issue concerns the role of existing community groups and institutions in neighborhood government. The question is: who benefits from decentralization? The objection was frequently made that neighborhood government was worthless if it was not designed explicitly to "strengthen existing units" (#4). This view is put simply by a Queens civic association, "There presently exists a very efficient community reaction whereby individuals, civic associations, ad hoc committees, etc. make their problems known to city administrators."

The corollary view is that neighborhood government would entail a foolish abandonment of long-standing community investments and efforts. "You're proposing that we lose everything we have here—three city offices and hardworking community groups and get very little in return." "Don't abolish what exists and works well just for the sake of creating something new."

Many of the arguments for strengthening existing institutions have the look of special pleading by established groups seeking to protect their domain. The advice of one community corporation official was to strengthen the corporations since "every function assigned to the new boards is presently being performed by community corporations." The advice of the Co-op City Advisory Council was to put the council in charge of neighborhood government. Finally, various city councilmen objected that neighborhood government should be built in the councilmen's office; and one noted that "all these neighborhood government plans" are simply ways of "interfering with the responsible work of duly elected officials." Members of the community boards, which are an arm of the borough president's office, argued frequently that more power should be given to the borough president (#12).

The second issue that provoked deep-seated conflict concerned the method of choosing representatives in neighborhood government (#1). Although the majority opinion was that citizens should be elected, there was sharp disagreement on election procedures. Some participants in the consultation argued that representatives be elected from small wards—"sharply circumscribed geographic areas within the district."

According to one Lower East Side community organization:

> Such a system would make slate-voting extremely difficult and would go a long way toward eliminating the kinds of abuses that occurred on the Lower East Side, at any rate, during the School Board election. During that election, a small corner of the community turned out by far the largest number of voters and elected a slate that was widely popular only in that corner.

As against this view, other participants argued strongly that neighborhood government would be impossible if it had to mediate between a large number of sharply focused local interests such as would be produced by a ward voting system.

More significant was the degree of sentiment against formal elections. According to one neighborhood activist, "this area can't stand another election after what has happened. It would be the straw that broke the camel's back." And in another view:

> Election of members should be vigorously *opposed*. It is a nostalgic effort to return to the town meeting of an agricultural society, where everyone knows everyone else, and is totally irrelevant to a modern urban metropolis. Citizens are already expected to exercise informed judgment in the election of about 60 judges and in the election of local school boards. To offer 100 candidates for 25 to 50 places on a community board will probably lead to ethnic voting, will require thoughtful citizens of the type now on the boards to stage political campaigns.

Those neighborhood residents who preferred an appointment process to formal elections often did so for negative reasons.

There does not seem to be sufficient motivation to induce qualified individuals to invest the time and funds necessary to win an election of this sort. We believe that the appointment process would yield a higher type of individual.

However, as before, proponents of the appointment process expressed different and often opposed ideas about how the process should work. Some wanted existing community groups to appoint neighborhood government representatives. But which groups? "Block associations," said several block association leaders—because they provide "direct" street-level government not "indirect on top of indirect." "Community corporations should be the basis," argued various corporation leaders. Still others argued for a "convention of established community organizations," but critics of this scheme did not want powerful established organizations to have "the final say" because they are variously thought to be "unrepresentative," "undemocratic," "controlled by narrow cliques who use their funds for patronage and do not work for the larger interests of the community."

Patterns of Opposition

The consultations also revealed several patterns of opposition based on social and organizational factors. Reactions from middle-class white neighborhoods emphasized the cost of neighborhood government and the fear of political interference by the mayor. The strongest reactions from poor, black neighborhoods were that the community was not given enough power and that the plan would not solve anything.

The organizational sources of opposition to the plan have been referred to above. The consultations show that myriad neighborhood organizations exist that feel threatened by any restructuring of neighborhood government. These established interests, be they neighborhood associations, community planning boards, or Model Cities advisory committees, want to be placed at the center of any new neighborhood plan and oppose initiatives that fail this test. Of course, these claims of primacy clashed sharply in neighborhoods where many such groups existed.

Further, different neighborhoods wanted to proceed toward neighborhood government at different rates and in different ways. Some community groups claimed they already had the kind of neighborhood government that the plan proposed and did not want to be bothered with new initiatives. Other neighborhood groups felt they were ready to move immediately to community control. Still others warned that at present the neighborhoods were too divided and disorganized to benefit from neighborhood government.

We have seen that different neighborhood organizations sought a decentralization plan that would strengthen their political positions. So do politicians proposing new decentralization plans. In the wake of the mayor's plan of 1970, other political officials have presented their own blueprints. The plans submitted by two borough presidents strengthen the role of that office.[7] A plan drafted by several city councilmen envisioned a new and central role for the councilmen.[8]

The Political Viability of Neighborhood Government

The evidence of the New York consultations suggests the following conclusions about the future of neighborhood government.[9]

1. Objections to specific plans will dissolve the apparent consensus of support for the idea of decentralization.
2. Objections to specific plans will be diverse and often contradictory.
3. The range of objections is such that any specific plan—mild or drastic—will evoke widespread dissent. But the more comprehensive the plan, the more interests are affected and the more widespread the objections are likely to be.
4. Citizens fear political encroachment in city hall initiatives and will be highly cynical about the possible benefits of any plan.
5. Existing neighborhood groups will feel threatened by any decentralization plan.
6. Neighborhood organization and leading politicians alike will try to shape decentralization plans to strengthen their political power.
7. Different neighborhoods will have different preferences and different capacities for neighborhood government.

In sum, the political viability of neighborhood government is tenuous, and one suspects that any coalition in support of any specific plan would be a fragile one. The more comprehensive the plan, the more fragile the coalition. Remembering too that any decentralization plan depends for its effectiveness on the consent of neighborhood interests, we can predict that attempts to achieve substantial decentralization will be costly in time and political energy. And if city politicians act "economically"—try to achieve the greatest amount of decentralization at the least political cost—we can predict further that future initiatives in neighborhood government will be taken in small, cautious steps. It is likely too that political leaders will prefer administrative decentralization to political decentralization since the former avoids the complications and turmoil of widespread citizen participation.

10 Decentralization, Development, and Democracy

In the final analysis, decentralization must be judged on its ability to produce neighborhood development and democracy. For it is the promise of achieving these objectives that makes decentralization an important and ambitious strategy. In terms of neighborhood development, we want to know what impact decentralization has had to date and what impact it might have under different conditions. We saw earlier that advocates believe decentralization will stimulate development by having four kinds of impacts: administrative, economic, psychological, and political. Assessing the decentralization experiments in terms of these hopes, we find that the administrative justification (decentralization will produce greater responsiveness) is most clearly supported by the evidence. The political justification (decentralization will stimulate leadership development and political efficacy) depends on whether decentralization experiments achieved tangible results. The psychological justification (decentralization will make citizens "feel closer" to government) cannot be assessed conclusively with available evidence. Many citizens were unaware of decentralization experiments in their neighborhoods, and these residents certainly do not feel any closer to government. In general, the psychological impact is likely to be at best a delayed effect of decentralization, a possible result of the long-term learning process. Finally, the experience of existing experiments does not support the economic justification (decentralization will produce more efficient resource allocation). The experiments simply did not have sufficient resources at their disposal to make the kinds of allocation decisions that might make for a more efficient use of resources.

For the future, we predict that the creation of new, service-oriented experiments will increase both the "administrative" impact and the "political" impact on leadership development and political efficacy. Under any conditions, the "psychological" impact will be uncertain and will take a long time to materialize; and the "economic" impact will not be realized until decentralization experiments gain control of substantial and flexible fiscal resources.

Assessing the impact of decentralization on different kinds of urban problems, we have found that "responsiveness" problems are most susceptible to treatment through decentralization. "Resource" problems were not affected at all. The impact on "trust" problems remains unclear. The community school board and the Hill Health Corporation may have improved the trust relationship between professionals and their citizen clients, but no conclusive evidence exists on this effect. Problems of "self-regulation" were affected marginally—only by block associations working directly at the grassroots. Finally, decentralization had no effect on "restructuring" problems—problems that required cooperation at the metropolitan, state, or federal level.

For the future we predict that decentralization is capable of having a substantial impact on responsiveness problems—especially if more focused, small-scale, experiments are developed. The impact on "trust" problems will increase if the learning process takes hold and if new experiments place street-level bureaucrats and neighborhood leaders in a cooperative relationship dealing with shared problems. The impact on problems of self-regulation will be increased only if decentralization experiments are developed which, like block associations, work directly with neighborhood residents at the street level. Finally, under no circumstances will decentralization have an impact on "restructuring" problems. If the main concern of public policy is to deal with problems like integration, pollution control, and the fiscal imbalance between urban and suburban school districts, there is no reason to invest political resources in decentralization.

Different Strategies, Different Neighborhoods

Not only do different decentralization strategies have different impacts, they also have different uses and limits. No decentralization does everything. Some achieve strong interest articulation, others strong interest aggregation. Some mobilize residents at the grassroots, others stimulate broad discussion of needs and problems. Some identify and solve concrete problems, others identify and struggle with more fundamental urban problems. Some experiments, like community boards, are well-suited to mount protests in times of crisis. Others, like the Community Task Force, work best on concrete problems on a day-to-day basis. Put another way, the structures of decentralization experiments are not infinitely elastic.[1] If no neighborhood structure can play every desirable role, the question becomes: what use does a neighborhood most want to make of decentralization and what kind of impact does it want to achieve? The answers to these questions depend on the nature of the neighborhood and on the degree of political development in the community.

For if decentralization strategies have different uses and limits, so also do neighborhoods have different needs and capabilities. Neighborhoods differ in racial, economic, and geographic characteristics as well as in leadership development, rootedness, and number of internal cleavages. Drawing on the experience of the seven experiments,[2] we can offer the following predictions about the likely relationship between decentralization strategies and neighborhood types. In general, the higher the income level in the neighborhood, the more it will emphasize service-oriented experiments. Also, the more developed the leadership in a neighborhood, the more it will favor focused experiments capable of achieving concrete results. Conversely, we would expect poor neighborhoods with weakly developed political leadership to produce sporadic protest activity and loosely-knit protest groups in the early stages of political development. Further, the greater the number of cleavages within a neighborhood (be they racial, ethnic, economic, or geographical), the more difficult it will be to develop viable, neighborhoodwide assemblies—indeed the more difficult it will be to develop any neighborhood institution. Conversely, the more homogeneous, affluent, and rooted the neighborhood and the greater the leadership development, the greater will be its capacity for comprehensive decentralization. No slight is intended against the poorest neighborhoods in this analysis. The point is simply that a neighborhood that is relatively affluent and has a developed leadership possesses vital political resources which poor, undeveloped neighborhoods lack. Moreover, in a community that has a relatively rooted population and few internal cleavages, the costs of community organization and institution building are far lower than in a divided, transient neighborhood. It is significant that this distinction does not necessarily hinge on racial differences. The analysis of block associations throughout New York City showed that many white neighborhoods were divided and undeveloped, while many nonwhite neighborhoods were relatively rooted, homogeneous, and developed.

If a neighborhood has a developed political leadership but is internally divided, decentralization experiments will tend to be dominated by established interests, and it will be very difficult to achieve a strong representation of new interests (be they racial, economic, or geographical). The implication of this analysis should be clear—indeed it has been a constant theme in this study. That is, no single decentralization strategy will work in every neighborhood. Stated positively, neighborhoods will benefit most from decentralization if experiments are carefully tailored to fit the particular needs and capacities of the neighborhood. This conclusion stands against the universalistic approach often favored by city hall and the federal government that seeks uniform solutions to urban problems.

The Sequence of Political Development

It is clear that different neighborhoods are in different stages of political development. What is less clear is what sequence, if any, the development process takes in urban neighborhoods, and, further, if there is a common sequence, what its implications are for decentralization. The authors of a recent study argue that development is characterized by a sequence of crises and demands on the political system.[3] According to Sydney Verba, these crises and demands relate most generally to the conflicting problems of "equality," "capacity," and "differentiation," and more specifically to several "performance areas," including "identity," "legitimacy," and "participation."[4] Recently, urban politics has also been characterized by a major crisis and by a resulting sequence of neighborhood demands and government responses. The crisis arose from the black demand for equality and social justice—a demand that was expressed in the civil rights movement, in neighborhood protests, and in the riots of the 1960s. In Verba's terms this was a crisis of "equality" and, more specifically, of "participation." The resulting sequence was as follows. After the crisis reached its peak in the middle 1960s, many black urban residents focused on the problem of political "identity,"[5] of developing a sense of community and political strength. Indeed, both the black power and community control movements expressed the determination of blacks to become a coherent and distinctive force in the political system. The response of government to the crisis and subsequent demands was to develop new opportunities for citizen participation—for example, in community action and Model Cities. Similarly, many city halls moved to strengthen the legitimacy of city government by decentralizing it. To this point, the sequence of neighborhood development was crisis (black protest and riots)—assertion of political "identity" (demands for community control) and government response (some decentralization and new opportunities for participation). In general, in the early stages of development, protest was the neighborhood's main weapon. Even if it was a limited weapon, it was the only weapon the neighborhoods possessed, and it produced the only victories neighborhoods were able to win.

The developmental sequence in urban neighborhoods was critically affected at this stage by the introduction of new institutions: the experiments in decentralization. For with the introduction of self-government, citizen demands shifted along with the shift in responsibility from city hall to the neighborhood. With neighborhood leaders working in neighborhood institutions, the main demands on the political system were for "capacity" and "legitimacy." Specifically, residents and leaders wanted neighborhood government to solve problems (capacity), to be representative of and accountable to residents (legitimacy). This is the obvious meaning of one Hill resident's angry comment about Model Cities, "The whole thing isn't worth a hill of beans. They don't do anything for us and they don't care what we feel. No neighborhood people would do the things they do. But we don't have any power at all . . . even though we're supposed to."

In short, my argument is that most urban neighborhoods are now at the stage of political development where capacity and legitimacy are the critical demands. And if this is true, the implications for decentralization are clear: experiments will have to be carefully designed and make concrete and visible impacts on neighborhood problems.

Although the experience of the seven experiments confirms the logic of this developmental sequence, it is necessary to qualify the thesis in two ways before relating it generally to the choice between different decentralization strategies.

First, not all urban neighborhoods have gone through the initial protest stage. In fact, it has only been very recently that many white "ethnic" neighborhoods have begun the sequence of protest and assertion of political identity. Undoubtedly, there are other neighborhoods that have not yet begun to mobilize at all and in which protest organizations rather than service-oriented experiments would be the most appropriate initiative. Also, because a neighborhood has passed beyond the first stage of protest does not mean that protest has become a useless tactic.

Protest and Political Development

As long as higher level governments hold dominant policymaking power, neighborhoods will often have to mount protests against decisions and programs that they oppose but do not control. But protest is a costly and frequently frustrating technique of political action. To sustain mass protest, leaders must keep residents mobilized for weeks or even months and must continually organize demonstrations and meetings with city officials. This takes time and energy, and it is harder to get the people out for the fifth demonstration than for the first. Also, as Lipsky has shown, city hall will usually stall, hold endless meetings, make studies, and be attentive (by giving residents a hearing) without being responsive.[6] In short, the costs of a protest to the neighborhood are high to begin with and grow higher if, as is likely, the city does not respond to neighborhoods demands. Further, protest leaders must not only bear the costs of political mobilization, they also have to deal with the frustrations of defeat and drift. It is no accident that the "protesters" in our leadership sample had very low efficacy scores and that most of the protest leaders in New Haven in the mid-sixties had been "burned out"–had drifted out of the city or out of neighborhood work.[7] The technique of protest has a further characteristic that affects its role in a strategy of neighborhood development. That is, protest is dependent on the existence of highly charged issues and events. If the bulldozers have arrived to begin tearing down housing for a highway, local leaders will have little difficulty in mounting a strong protest. But much government policymaking is invisible to residents–however much it affects their interests. Also, many fundamental neighborhood problems–education, housing, and unemployment–are notable for their inexorability, not for producing the sudden explosions and controversies best suited to protest activity. For these reasons, protest is usually both spontaneous and limited–spontaneous because it relies on the appearance of burning issues that immediately jolt residents into action, limited because only a few problems develop in this way.

To summarize, protest remains an important ingredient in any strategy of neighborhood development. But because of its limits and frustrations, it is not sufficient as a strategy for neighborhood problem-solving. The creation of service-oriented institutions does not eliminate the need for protest; rather it adds another dimension to the development strategy and also strengthens the neighborhood's capacity for sustained protest by expanding its organizational base. Most important, because protests will often arise spontaneously when the necessary conditions exist, it is somewhat redundant to build protest-oriented institutions after the initial stage of mobilization has been reached. Aside from the fact that such institutions cannot meet the growing demands for capacity and legitimacy, they will at best be one-dimensional and at worst ineffectual. Also, as the community action experience illustrates, neighborhood institutions created by government to fight government are likely to produce strong resentment and resistance among city officials.[8]

A Strategy of Development

To this point, my analysis of decentralization experiments has pointed implicitly to a strategy of neighborhood development. We will now make that strategy explicit by stating its central assumptions, outlining its features, and showing how it might develop over time.

The strategy depends on four assumptions: (1) focused, service-oriented experiments are most likely to have an initial impact on neighborhood problems and to increase the sense of political efficacy in the neighborhood. (2) Decentralization experiments have different uses and limits and neighborhoods have different needs and capacities. Strategies of decentralization must therefore be tailored to fit the neighborhood; it must be pluralistic not uniform. (3) In the process of development, neighborhood residents will move from demands for participation and political "identity" to demands for capacity and legitimacy. (4) Protest is a crucial element in any development strategy, but it is not sufficient. Protest is likely to arise spontaneously, and it will be strengthened by the existence of successful, service-oriented institutions.

In broad outline, the strategy that best fits these assumptions emphasizes self-help, ombudsmen, and neighborhood service center models of decentralization. It avoids—at least at first—the "governments-in-miniature" model. The strategy of creating a pluralistic structure of service-oriented neighborhood experiments is, as Hirschman puts it, a strategy of "unbalanced growth."[9] Rather than developing a comprehensive neighborhood government, this strategy seeks to capitalize on existing "growth points" that will yield high "profits" or, in our terms, tangible results. The strategy also depends on the assumption that certain highly visible successes will stimulate neighborhood leadership and have two kinds of "spillover" effects. First, the creation of effective block associations or ombudsman structures in one part of the neighborhood will lead to imitation elsewhere in the neighborhood. More important, the first-generation experiments will not be static but will evolve into broader-based institutions with wider initiatives. The expectation is that self-help organizations like block associations will expand their constituencies and develop day care centers, education programs, and the like; that ombudsman structures will take on a wider range of "complaints"; and that neighborhood-run service centers will add new services. More concretely, evidence that this evolution can take place exists in the experiment of the Hill Health Corporation, which gradually expanded its services and clientele, and in the experience of the Fairhaven Neighborhood Corporation, which moved from handling complaints to create a day care center, health clinic, and housing maintenance program. As the range and diversity of neighborhood institutions increase in this process of "unbalanced growth," cooperation and consolidation could begin to take place between the separate institutions. Ultimately, a neighborhoodwide institution might be created on a federal structure, with representatives of existing organizations serving in a kind of neighborhood senate.

The purpose of this strategy is simply to build durable foundations for neighborhood government at the street level. Because it starts with small-scale experiments, the strategy avoids the complexities and unmanageable responsibilities faced, for example, by the community school boards. In fact, on this strategy, governing boards could be created for individual schools but not for large districts. Further, this strategy is built on a succession of tangible impacts. It avoids the kind of decentralization that gives the appearance but not the substance of neighborhood government. The corollary to this strategy is that city hall must decentralize its administration so as to give neighborhood groups needed leverage, communication, and cooperation.

The Strategy Considered: Some Theoretical Perspectives

There are also several theoretical reasons for choosing a strategy of "unbalanced growth."

1. Choice. In his theory of political development, David Apter emphasizes the importance of "expanding choice,"[10] of creating a political system that provides alternatives in allocation and action. The strategy outlined above has precisely this result, for it involves a multiplicity of experiments offering different kinds of participation in different policy areas. In contrast, any comprehensive plan for neighborhood government is essentially monolithic—it presents the citizen with only one mechanism for participation. In our strategy, the citizen is offered a range of opportunities and can match his own background and leadership style with the purposes and needs of different decentralization experiments. The entrepreneur can pursue his own style of activism, the ombudsman his, and so forth. Indeed, since the structure of neighborhood institutions strongly shapes the leadership style of neighborhood politicians, different experiments with different orientations must exist if different leadership styles and skills are to develop.

2. Incrementalism. Charles Lindblom has argued that decisionmaking inevitably takes place in a context of uncertainty and bounded rationality.[11] He presents a "strategy of decision," incrementalism, that involves lower costs in information getting and analysis and that seeks to solve large problems by making a series of small, sequential steps. Whatever the utility of Lindblom's strategy in the context of the federal government or city hall, it does speak directly to the problems of neighborhood institutions. For as we have seen, neighborhood leaders typically lack time, information, and administrative expertise. They have to get a program going and make an impact if their institutions are to survive. Conversely, we have seen in the experience of the community school boards, community boards, and some neighborhood corporations how frustrating and futile when neighborhood institutions attempt a comprehensive, "synoptic" approach to a wide range of problems. In short, our strategy of unbalanced growth is incremental not in the sense that it is interested only in small impacts, but in that it involves focused and thus bounded decisionmaking on concrete service problems. Not every problem is taken on; it is a strategy of suboptimization. The strategy is also incremental in that it entails a process of development in which neighborhood experiments "erode" local problems through a series of successes that increase in magnitude as the neighborhood's sense of political efficacy grows.

3. The Logic of Collective Action.[12] There are two aspects of the logic of collective action that bear on our strategy. First, we know that it is often impossible for one individual to attack local problems if other members of the community do not join with him in collective action or self-regulation. For example, a rent strike cannot be organized if most tenants are unwilling to participate, and also it is impossible to clean up a block if only a minority of residents agree to stop littering or dumping their garbage on the street. In this respect the logic of collective action is that large numbers of residents must be mobilized and organized if community action is to work. On the other hand, Olson and others have shown that smaller groups are likely to be more effective than large ones in mounting and sustaining collective action.[13] Thus, we have the apparent contradiction that successful collective action in the neighborhood setting depends on the local group being both small and large. Seen in these terms, the formal comprehensive model of decentralization appears to have the worst of both worlds: large representative assemblies with shallow roots in the neighborhoods. By contrast, the strategy of unbalanced growth solves this problem—as far as it is possible to do so—by creating many small experiments that work directly with neighborhood residents. In fact, block associations come closest to resolving the contradiction in collective action by developing small, coherent leadership groups *and* widespread participation among block residents.

4. Reforms as Experiments. As has been noted above, we do not know what impact and success decentralization experiments will have. We do not have enough experience with decentralization experiments to make ironclad predictions of success or failure. For this reason decentralization initiatives continue to be experiments; and indeed, according to Donald Campbell, all reforms are inevitably experiments.[14] If this is true, it is strongly in the interests of city hall *and* the neighborhoods to test a variety of different initiatives so as to see what structures work and also to avoid gambling all their resources on one investment. Seen in these terms, the strategy of "unbalanced growth" is desirable because it involves a diversity of experiments.

5. Voice and Exit. Decentralization is, in part, a response to the belief that existing institutions are rigidified, unresponsive, and unrepresentative. Looking to the future, it is equally possible that neighborhood institutions will atrophy and lose citizen support. As Hirschman has argued, the normal response to decline in political organization is either "voice" (or protest), but the optimal response is a combination of "voice" and "exit."[15] However, if one comprehensive neighborhood government were established, it would be apt to become quickly entrenched and difficult to change or terminate except through protest. On the other hand, the creation of small, diversified experiments mitigates this problem in two ways. First, the more small-scale and service-oriented the experiment the clearer and more visible its success or failure is likely to be. More important, the smaller the experiment the less entrenched it is likely to be since there are smaller "sunk costs" and fewer people whose livelihood depends on the survival of the experiment. Under these conditions, the likelihood that "exit" will be a response to decline in neighborhood institutions is greatly increased. With a strategy of small, experimental initiatives, neighborhood leaders and residents alike can stop participating or supporting a program in the face of clear failure without eliminating their only opportunities for community action. Some evidence that the "exit" response will occur under these conditions is found in the experience of block associations where organizations appear and disappear regularly in response to perceptions of opportunity and decline.

The Politics of Neighborhood Development

The future of any decentralization strategy depends both on political trends within the city and on the nature of federal policy toward the city. Specifically, the demand for decentralization arose in nonwhite neighborhoods, and minority group demands remain an important source of political pressure and support for new decentralization initiatives. However, it is by no means clear that minority group communities will continue to fight for decentralization. This is because citizen participation in urban government points in two directions. One kind of participation is *centrifugal* and involves a division of central government functions and powers such that the neighborhoods can increase their power and control. The other kind of participation is centripetal, and, in this form, neighborhood groups seek increased control of central government. The first form of participation was typified by the Ocean Hill-Brownsville leaders and the second form by those political movements led by Carl Stokes, Ralph Hatcher, and Kenneth Gibson that led to the election of black mayors. The choice between these forms of participation is in large part a function of numbers. The black population of New York was nowhere near an electoral majority—the black population in Newark was (as it was in Cleveland and Gary). On the basis of this experience and of political logic, we would predict that in those cities where the nonwhite population is below 30 percent demands for decentralization will continue to be strong. In cities where the nonwhite population approaches a majority (40 percent and over), political energies will be devoted to capturing city hall.

Inevitably, policies of the federal government will have a strong impact on the future of decentralization strategies. Although the federal government presently has no urban policy, much less a neighborhood policy, the decisions that are made nationally on revenue sharing, income maintenance, and categorical aid programs will powerfully affect the climate for decentralization in the cities. Our strategy depends, in part, on the existence of service-oriented initiatives such as neighborhood health centers and multiservice centers, which typically have been funded by the federal government. To the extent that funds presently allocated to service-oriented experiments are withdrawn or channeled into income maintenance or general revenue sharing, the prospects for a strategy of unbalanced growth are diminished. Conversely, the more federal funds that are allocated to service-oriented experiments, the stronger the foundations for this decentralization strategy will be.

Decentralization and Democracy

If decentralization experiments are capable of stimulating neighborhood development, their ability to achieve neighborhood democracy is more problematic. As we saw in Chapter 5, no decentralization experiment came close to meeting the various tests of democratic process. Taking a more theoretical perspective, we can draw several broad conclusions from existing experience about the relationship between decentralization and democracy. First, decentralization experiments unquestionably create more direct democracy than has existed before in American cities. Even in the relatively unsuccessful initiatives, more neighborhood residents participate and have a more powerful role to play than ever before. More significantly, the participation created by decentralization in many American cities constitutes a greater degree of direct democracy than exists in local government in any western democracy. In many European countries, as we have seen, the political system is highly centralized. And even in those western democracies where local government appears to play a relatively strong role, mechanisms for direct citizen participation usually do not exist. Urban residents may vote regularly in Switzerland and England, but they do not participate directly in their governance either at the town hall or the neighborhood level.

At the same time, the experience of existing experiments reveals the limits of decentralization in achieving direct democracy. There has been considerable debate about the relationship between community size and democracy. Some analysts have argued that participatory democracy cannot exist in communities larger than 150,000,[16] although Altshuler and other decentralization advocates are perfectly content to experiment on a larger scale. Others have set a far lower figure as the outer limit for direct democracy. The evidence presented above indicates that only in block associations—with a "community size" of several hundred—did widespread citizen participation occur. Strong participation was also achieved in the Hill Health Corporation, but again the community was small—a consumer population of several thousand. Conversely, in the neighborhoodwide experiments—both in small New Haven communities of 10-15,000 and large New York communities of over 10,000—citizen participation rarely exceeded the 5-10 percent range in neighborhood elections. The implication of this experience is clear: decentralization can substantially strengthen direct democracy, but it will not achieve the town meeting ideal of participatory democracy unless the community involved is extremely small.

Decentralization experiments also provide stronger "social representation" than existed before although that representation is imperfect, and "new interests" are often weakly represented. In particular, decentralization experiments typically give strong representation to established community interests and thus give additional leverage to existing neighborhood groups. Clearly, this effect of decentralization is double-edged, for the strengthening of existing interests constrains the development of underrepresented and unrepresented interests.

A third effect of decentralization is that it increases pluralism in urban democracy. In promoting "local solutions" to neighborhood problems, decentralization permits the articulation of more diverse preferences and interests and thus enhances local self-determination.

To this point, it would appear decentralization contributes strongly to urban democracy, but there are more issues involved than participation, representation, and pluralism. As we have seen, critics of decentralization often make their case in the name of democratic values. In my judgment, some of these objections are misplaced, although others raise serious problems. Two frequent objections are that neighborhood government will lead to tyranny by either the local majority or local minorities and will further fragment an already badly fragmented political system.

The experience of the seven experiments does not confirm the tyranny arguments. Not only was there almost no evidence of monopolistic control by either local minorities or majorities, but, in fact, just the opposite pattern obtained. Widespread internal conflict was the dominant characteristic of neighborhood governance.

The fragmentation argument cannot be answered empirically because decentralization obviously does fragment urban government. The larger question is: should fragmentation be viewed as an important problem when the rest of the political system is already hopelessly fragmented? If urban decentralization was the only obstacle to a "rational" restructuring of American political institutions, the problem of fragmentation would indeed be crucial. But this is not the case. Therefore, to oppose urban decentralization on the grounds of fragmentation is to impose a discriminatory standard on neighborhood democracy—a standard that is especially unfair if, as a result, neighborhoods are deprived of the benefits of fragmentation that suburbs and other jurisdictions commonly enjoy. A more substantial objection is that decentralization, because it fragments policies and procedures, undermines basic standards of due process.[17] This may well prove true in practice, but in principle this is not a necessary result of decentralization. Just as central government audits can be used to enforce minimum standards in spending and accounting, so higher level legislation can establish basic individual rights and protections. Decentralization does not entail the deliberate abandonment of civil liberties. It is again a question of how decentralization experiments are structured.

More serious objections to decentralization which are confirmed by our evidence are that neighborhood institutions often do not provide strong, formal mechanisms of accountability nor do they adhere faithfully to democratic procedures in decisionmaking. In addition, to the extent that neighborhood institutions articulate and act on their own parochial interests, there is a clear tension between neighborhood democracy and the public interest. This tension is most likely to arise when the central government seeks to locate necessary but unpopular public facilities—such as a sewage treatment plant, half-way house, or low-income housing—in some neighborhood in the city. In this case, and in others like it, what is good for any given neighborhood is not good for the city.

More important, decentralization creates two serious dilemmas for the democratic theorist. First, decentralization evokes a familiar conflict between the values of equal treatment and social justice. If higher level governments allocate funds equally to different neighborhoods, the goal of equal treatment is advanced, but the desire for social justice which recognizes the special needs of poor, nonwhite neighborhoods is not furthered. Second, there is a clear and disturbing conflict in neighborhood democracy between the quest for community and the desire for racial integration. The importance of strengthening urban communities—of giving city dwellers a sense of rootedness, cohesion, and social identity—is by now a platitude in American political discourse. But the quest for community clearly has its price. Almost all the neighborhood leaders interviewed believed that decentralization would reinforce existing patterns of racial segregation. Black leaders wanted to build strong black communities, white leaders wanted to build (or protect) strong white ones. Few leaders opposed integration in principle, but the logic of neighborhood democracy led them to emphasize different, conflicting priorities. In short, decentralization does not and cannot fulfill every democratic value because those values are often in sharp conflict. The question becomes one of choosing which values matter most. If we choose participation, representation, pluralism, and community, we can conclude the decentralization will indeed foster neighborhood democracy.

In conclusion, the message of this study is that decentralization is a hopeful and viable alternative in urban policy. Most important, decentralization holds the promise of creating more direct democracy than has ever existed before in American cities. The question for the future is not whether decentralization should be pursued but rather what kind of decentralization should be initiated. Drawing on the experience of existing experiments, we have presented a strategy of decentralization that appears to fulfill certain observed, structural conditions of success in neighborhood institutions. It is now necessary to convert decentralization from a fighting word into an effective public policy.

Notes

Notes

Notes to Chapter 1
Decentralization in Urban Politics

1. These innovations take many different forms including little city halls, neighborhood service centers, citizen advisory boards, community corporations, Model Cities, neighborhood health centers, and decentralized school boards.

2. Milton Kotler, *Neighborhood Government* (New York: Bobbs-Merrill, 1969). Earlier, Kotler outlined his case for the creation of neighborhood corporations in "Two Essays on the Neighborhood Corporation," in *Urban America: Goals and Problems*, Joint Economic Committee, Subcommittee on Urban Affairs, Washington, 1967, pp. 170-91. A well-reasoned blueprint for decentralization is found in Richard Danzig and Benjamin W. Heineman, Jr., "Decentralization in New York City: A Proposal," *Harvard Journal of Legislation*, March 1971, pp. 407-54. The most cogent presentation of the arguments for community control of schools is Mario Fantini, Marilyn Gittell, and Richard Magat, *Community Control and the Urban School* (New York: Praeger, 1970).

3. Alan Altshuler, *Community Control* (New York: Pegasus, 1970). Other general assessments of the decentralization question are Donna E. Shalala, *Neighborhood Governance–Issues and Proposals*, a report for the National Project on Ethnic America, American Jewish Committee, 1971 and three symposia:

a. Henry M. Levin (ed.), *Community Control of Schools* (New York: Clarion, 1970);

b. "Symposium on Neighborhoods and Citizen Involvement" *Public Administration Review*, No. 3, May/June 1972;

c. Bruce Smith and George La Noue (eds.), "Urban Decentralization and Community Participation" in *American Behavioral Scientist* 15, 1, (Sept./Oct. 1971).

4. The published material on Ocean Hill-Brownsville is too extensive to review in full here. Among the most informative and evocative studies are: Maurice Berube and Marilyn Gittell (eds.), *Confrontation at Ocean Hill-Brownsville* (New York: Prager, 1969); Marilyn Gittell, "Education, the Decentralization–Community School Controversy" in Jewel Bellush and Stephen David (eds.), *Race and Politics in New York City* (New York, Praeger, 1971); and Naomi Levine, *Ocean Hill-Brownsville: A Case History of Schools in Crisis* (New York: Popular Library, 1969).

5. The reports of the Center for Governmental Studies provide a useful inventory and brief analysis of existing decentralization experiments. See especially the following: *Neighborhood Facilities and Municipal Decentralization*, Washington, D.C., 1971, 2 vols.; Howard Hallman, *Community Corpora-*

tions and Neighborhood Control, 1970; and George Washnis, *Little City Halls*, 1970. See also Eric Nordlinger, "Decentralizing the American City: A Case Study of Boston's Little City Halls" (unpublished manuscript); and Howard Hallman, *Neighborhood Control of Public Programs* (New York: Praeger, 1970).

6. The I.S. 201 experience is analyzed in Miriam Wasserman, *The School Fix* (New York, Outerbridge and Dienstfrey, 1970), pp. 211-307, and in David Rogers, *110 Livingston Street* (New York, Random House, 1968), pp. 29-30, 364-70.

7. Michael Lipsky, *Protest in City Politics* (Chicago: Rand McNally, 1970).

8. The origins of the community action program have been widely analyzed. Three useful treatments of the development of community action are Peter Marris and Martin Rein, *Dilemmas of Social Reform* (New York, Atherton, 1967); Daniel P. Moynihan, *Maximum Feasible Misunderstanding* (New York, The Free Press, 1969): and John C. Donovan, *The Politics of Poverty* (New York: Pegasus, 1967).

9. Pointing to the community action program and the existence of myriad other neighborhood organizations, Bell comments that there may be "more participation than ever before in American society, particularly in the large urban centers such as New York, and more opportunity for the active and interested person to express his political and social concerns." Daniel Bell and Virginia Held, "The Community Revolution," in *The Public Interest*. No. 16, Summer 1969, p. 142.

10. See Charles Adrian and Charles Press, *Governing Urban America* (New York: McGraw-Hill, 1965), pp. 241-61.

11. Over 60 percent of all cities of over 5,000 elect all of their city councilmen at-large.

12. For a general treatment of the careers of these two men, see Jeanne Lowe, *Cities in a Race with Time* (New York: Harper and Row, 1967). Moses reflects his own career as a "master builder" in *Public Works: A Dangerous Trade* (New York: McGraw-Hill, 1970). Lee's development of an "executive-centered coalition" is analyzed in Robert Dahl, *Who Governs?* (New Haven: Yale University Press, 1961).

13. This analysis draws on the discussion of public goods in economic theory although the classification of public goods presented here is my own interpretation. For a discussion and critique of the way the concept of public goods is used in economic analysis, see Peter A. Steiner, "The Public Sector and the Public Interest" in Robert Haveman and Julius Margolis (eds.), *Public Expenditure and Public Analysis* (Chicago: Markham, 1970), pp. 21-58.

14. Differences in income, geography, density, housing characteristics and life style are among the main factors that produce differences in need and demand for services both between and within different urban neighborhoods.

15. James Q. Wilson, *Varieties of Police Behavior* (Cambridge: Harvard University Press, 1968), p. 7.

16. Michael Lipsky, "Toward a Theory of Streetlevel Bureaucracy," Paper presented at the annual meeting of the American Political Science Association, 1969.

17. The fact that election turnout tends to be low in city elections—and especially in cities with a mayor-council form of government and partisan elections—is documented in Robert R. Alford and Eugene C. Lee, "Voting Turnout in Cities," *American Political Science Review* 62 (September 1968): 768-814.

18. This claim was made most notably by Daniel P. Moynihan in *Maximum Feasible Misunderstanding* (New York: The Free Press, 1969).

19. This claim is made by almost every advocate of decentralization. See Altshuler, *Community Control*, and Kotler, *Neighborhood Government*.

20. This claim underlies much of the case for community control of schools. See Fantini, Gittell, and Magat, *Community Control and the Urban School*.

21. Again, this claim is made by almost every advocate of decentralization. It is a claim that advocates virtually have to make if they want decentralization to be viewed as a hopeful alternative to the status quo.

Notes to Chapter 2
Powers to the Neighborhoods: The Background of an Idea

1. Mailer's position on neighborhood government is recorded in detail in Peter Manso (ed.), *Running Against the Machine* (Garden City, N.J.: Doubleday, 1969).

2. See Report of the Mayor's Advisory Panel on Decentralization of the New York City Schools, *Reconnection for Learning*, November 9, 1967.

3. Cited in Eric Nordlinger, "Decentralizing the American City: A Study of Boston's Little City Halls," unpublished manuscript, p. 49.

4. See Mayor John V. Lindsay, *A Plan for Neighborhood Government*, 1970.

5. Altshuler, *Community Control*. The quotation is the subtitle of the book.

6. The NAACP resolution is noted in Nordlinger, "Decentralizing the American City," p. 22.

7. *New York Times*, July 6, 1969.

8. Advisory Commission on Intergovernmental Relations, *Urban America and the Federal System* (Washington: U.S. Govt. Printing Office, 1969), p. 96.

9. Report of the National Advisory Commission on Civil Disorders (New York, Bantam Books, 1968), pp. 295-96.

10. Report of the National Commission on Urban Problems (Washington, D.C.: U.S. Govt. Printing Office, 1968), pp. 350-53.

11. Association of the Bar, "A Discussion Draft: For a Symposium on Decentralizing New York City Government" (New York, Association of the Bar of the City of New York, 1970).

12. Irving Kristol, "Decentralization for What?" *The Public Interest*, November 11, 1968, p. 19.

13. Herbert Kaufman, "Administrative Decentralization and Political Power, *Public Administration Review* 29, 1 (January/February 1969): 6.

14. Ibid.

15. Ibid., p. 3.

16. Ibid.

17. Cited in Anwar Syed, *The Political Theory of American Local Government* (New York: Random House, 1966), p. 40.

18. Ibid., p. 44.

19. Ibid., p. 44.

20. See Ernest Griffith, *History of American City Government: The Colonial Period* (New York: Oxford University Press, 1936). Also his *Modern Development of City Government* (London: Oxford University Press, 1927).

21. Griffith, *History*, p. 194.

22. Ibid., p. 208.

23. Ibid., p. 211.

24. Ibid., pp. 211-212.

25. Ibid., p. 179.

26. Griffith, *Modern Development*, p. 25.

27. Ibid.

28. James Parton, "The Government of the City of New York," *North American Review* 102 (1866): 455-56.

29. The reference is to George Washington Plunkitt's famous remark: "I seen my opportunities and I took 'em." See William L. Riordan, *Plunkitt of Tammany Hall* (New York: Dutton, 1963).

30. Jerome Mushkat, *Tammany* (Syracuse, Syracuse University Press, 1971), pp. 364-65.

31. See Seymour J. Mandelbaum, *Boss Tweed's New York* (New York: Wiley, 1965).

32. For a full discussion of the political careers of the bosses, see Harold Zink, *City Bosses in the United States* (Dunham: Duke University Press, 1930).

33. Robert K. Merton, "The Latent Functions of the Machine," in Merton, *Social Theory and Social Structure* (New York: The Free Press, 1957), Rev. enl. ed., p. 72.

34. Ralph Martin, *The Bosses* (New York: Putnam, 1964), pp. 25-26.

35. For a first-hand account of these district leaders at the height of their powers, see Louis Eisenstein and Elliot Rosenberg, *A Stripe of Tammany's Tiger* (New York, Speller and Sons, 1966).

36. Samuel P. Hays, "The Politics of Reform in Municipal Government in the

Progressive Era," in Alexander B. Callow, Jr. (ed.), *American Urban History* (New York: Oxford University Press, 1969), p. 435.

37. Ibid., p. 431.

38. Ibid., p. 429.

39. Milton Kotler, *Neighborhood Government*, p. 19.

40. Mary Parker Follett, *The New State* (New York: Longmans, 1918), pp. 73-74.

41. For a discussion of Dewey's views, see Morton White and Lucia White, *The Intellectual Versus the City* (New York: Mentor, 1964), pp. 171-79.

42. Robert E. Park and Herbert Miller, *Old World Traits Transplanted* (New York: Harper and Bros., 1921), pp. 294-95.

43. Edward Banfield and James Wilson, *City Politics* (Cambridge: Harvard University Press, 1965), p. 192.

44. See Forbes Hayes, *Community Leadership: The Regional Plan Association of New York* (New York: Columbia University Press, 1965).

45. James Dahir, *The Neighborhood Unit Plan: Its Spread and Acceptance* (New York: Russell Sage Foundation, 1947), p. 5.

46. See Paul Goodman and Percival Goodman, *Communitas* (New York: Random House, 1947).

47. Lewis Mumford, *The Urban Prospect* (London: Secker and Warburg, 1968), p. 73.

48. See Dahir, *Neighborhood Unit Plan*.

49. See Morton White and Lucia White, *Intellectual Vs. City*, pp. 150-58.

50. Ibid., pp. 159-71.

51. For an analysis of the Home Rule debate in urban politics see Anwar Syed, *Political Theory*, p. 76 ff.

52. For a discussion of this and other Alinsky projects, see Marion K. Sanders, *The Professional Radical: Conversations with Saul Alinsky* (New York: Harper and Row, 1970).

53. Lawrence J.R. Herson, "The Lost World of Municipal Government," *American Political Science Review* 51 (1957): 330-45.

54. Robert Wood, *Suburbia* (New York: Houghton Mifflin, 1958), pp. 297-98.

55. Wallace S. Sayre and Herbert Kaufman, *Governing New York City* (New York: Norton, 1965).

56. Dahl, *Who Governs* (New Haven: Yale University Press, 1961), pp. 115-40.

57. "Citizen Participation in Urban Renewal," *Wisconsin Law Review* 66 (March 1966): 491-92.

58. Langley C. Keyes, Jr., *The Rehabilitation Planning Game* (Cambridge, MIT Press, 1969), p. 5. See also Harold Kaplan, *Urban Renewal Politics* (New York: Columbia University Press, 1963).

59. See J. Clarence Davies, *Neighborhood Groups and Urban Renewal* (New York: Columbia University Press, 1966).

60. Jane Jacobs, *The Death and Life of Great American Cities* (New York: Random House, 1961); and Herbert Gans, *The Urban Villagers* (New York: Free Press, 1962).

61. For a discussion of the origins and development of Community Progress, Inc. (CPI), see Kenneth Clark and Jeanette Hopkins, *A Relevant War Against Poverty*, (New York: Harper and Row, 1968), pp. 134-49; Fred Powledge, *Model City* (New York: Simon and Shuster, 1970); and Russell Murphy, *Political Entrepreneurs and Urban Poverty*, (New York: D.C. Health, 1971).

62. See Marris and Rein, *Dilemmas of Social Reform*, and Melvin Mogulof, "Coalition to Adversary: Citizen Participation in Three Federal Programs," *Journal of the American Institute of Planners*, July 1969, pp. 225-44.

63. Housing and Redevelopment Board, City of New York, *Neighborhood Conservation in New York City*, October 1966, p. 11.

64. See James V. Cunningham, *The Resurgent Neighborhood*, (Notre Dame, Indiana: Fides Publishers, 1965).

65. Ibid.

66. Moynihan, *Maximum Feasible Misunderstanding*, (New York: The Free Press, 1969).

67. See Sanford Kravitz, "The Community Action Program–Past, Present, and Its Future?" in James C. Sundquist (ed.), *On Fighting Poverty* (New York: Basic Books, 1968), pp. 52-70; and his "The Community Action Program in Perspective" in Warner Bloomberg and Henry Schmandt (eds.), *Power, Poverty, and Urban Policy*, (Beverly Hills: Sage Publications, 1968), pp. 259-83.

68. Richard Cloward, "The War on Poverty–Are the Poor Left Out?" in Chaim Waxman (ed.), *Poverty: Power and Politics* (New York: Grosset and Dunlap, 1968), pp. 159-70.

69. The Brandeis University Study, "Community Representation in 20 Cities" in Edgar Cahn and Barry Passett (eds.), *Citizen Participation* (Trenton, New Jersey Community Action Training Institute, 1970), p. 130. This finding is corroborated by extensive research on community action in other cities. See David Austin, "Resident Participation: Political Mobilization or Organizational Cooptation?" Discussion Paper, National Academy of Public Administration conference on Participation of the Poor and Public Administration (Holly Knoll, Virginia, 1970), pp. 23-24; Howard Hallman, "The Community Action Program: An Interpretive Analysis" in Bloomberg and Schmandt, *Power, Poverty, and Urban Policy*, pp. 285-311, unpublished Ford Foundation paper, 1967, p. 35.

70. See Ralph Kramer, *Participation of the Poor* (Englewood Cliffs, N.J.: Prentice Hall, 1969).

71. Sar Levitan, *The Great Society's Poor Law* (Baltimore: Johns Hopkins Press, 1969), p. 114.

72. U.S. Department of Housing and Urban Development, Improving the Quality of Urban Life (Washington, HUD, 1967), p. 20.

73. Mogulof, "Coalition to Adversary," p. 230. In general, existing evidence

suggests that city hall controls Model Cities programs, and neighborhoods play a limited role. See Roland L. Warren, "Model Cities First Round: Politics, Planning, and Participation," *Journal of the American Institute of Planners* 35 (July 1969): 246; Hans Spiegel and Stephen Mittenthal, *Neighborhood Power and Control*, (New York: Institute of Urban Environment, Columbia University, 1968), pp. 67-74.

74. Fantini, Gittell, and Magat, *Community Control and the Urban School*, (New York: Praeger, 1970), pp. 77-99.

75. See Lipsky, *Protest in City Politics.*

Notes to Chapter 3
Decentralization:
An Analytical Framework

1. James Fesler, "Approaches to the Understanding of Decentralization," *Journal of Politics* 27 (1965): 536.

2. Albert Reiss, *The Police and the Public* (New Haven: Yale University Press, 1971), pp. 173-221.

3. See Michael Lipsky, *Protest in City Politics*. Another volume, John Turner (ed.), *Neighborhood Organization for Community Action* (New York: National Association of Social Workers) reviews the role of "community self-help organizations." One author comments that self-help organizations "tend to deal with specific, immediate problems," p. 14.

4. "According to OEO estimates, as of October 1, 1968, there were approximately 1,000 neighborhood advisory councils throughout the nation on one or another aspect of the poverty program." The quotation is from "Decentralization to Neighborhoods: A Conceptual Analysis," an internal staff paper from the National Advisory Council on Economic Opportunity, published in 1968.

5. This figure is reported in one of the recent reports of the Center for Governmental Studies. See George J. Washnis, *Neighborhood Facilities and the Municipal Decentralization, Vol. I, Comparative Analysis of Twelve Cities* (Washington, D.C.: Center for Governmental Studies, 1971).

6. See Washnis, ibid., for a general review of ombudsman experiment. For an analysis of Boston's little city halls, see Nordlinger, "Decentralizing the American City: A Case Study of Boston's Little City Halls," (unpublished manuscript).

7. See Washnis, *Neighborhood Facilities*, p. 78.

8. Ibid., p. 117.

9. See Mogulof, "Coalition to Adversary: Citizen Participation in Three Federal Programs," *Journal of the American Institute of Planners*, July 1969, pp. 225-44.

10. See Howard W. Hallman, "Community Corporations and Neighborhood Control," Center for Governmental Studies, Pamphlet No. 1, Washington, D.C., 1970.

11. For a discussion of the origins and development of neighborhood health centers, see Wendy Brooks, "Health-Health Care and Poor People," in Edgar Cahn and Barry Passett (eds.) *Citizen Participation* (Trenton, New Jersey Community Action Training Institute, 1970); and James W. David, "Decentralization, Citizen Participation, and Ghetto Health Care," in Smith and La Noue (eds.) "Urban Decentralization and Community Participation" in *American Behavioral Scientist* 15, 1 (Sept./Oct. 1971).

12. Center for Governmental Studies, "Community Participation in Public Elementary Schools: A Survey Report"–mimeographed paper, Washington, 1970, p. 2.

Notes to Chapter 4
Initiatives and Impacts

1. Operation Better Block was sponsored by the city of New York and the Bristol Myers Company. The program "provides a small financial grant to help a neighborhood group organize and carry out a local improvement project. Neighborhood groups are assisted with field workers, briefing sessions, literature, and a special resource panel. This panel, comprised of artists, architects, landscape gardeners, representatives of municipal departments, as well as labor and community leaders, help block leaders get the needed help to improve a neighborhood." This description contained in pamphlet *Operation Better Block* published by the cosponsors in 1971.

2. Unless otherwise noted, all descriptive material on block associations comes from the files of the Office of Neighborhood Government, New York City. Unless otherwise noted, all direct quotations in this chapter are from interviews with neighborhood leaders and residents conducted by the author.

3. This newspaper, published in Bay Ridge, Brooklyn, contains a weekly column called "Block Association Notes," written by Judith Coyle Bush. The author interviewed Miss Bush several times to clarify certain aspects of block association activity in Brooklyn. The "Notes" column in the *Home Reporter and Sunset News* covers block associations in most of western Brooklyn.

4. *New York Times*, September 9, 1971.

5. Ibid., January 28, 1971.

6. Ibid.

7. Ibid.

8. Ibid, March 7, 1971.

9. Ibid., January 28, 1971.

10. Ibid.

11. Minutes of Community Board #3, October 22, 1963.

12. Minutes of Community Board #3, December 22, 1964.

13. This report and those that follow are taken from the files of the Ridgewood Community Task Force.

14. *New Haven Register*, April 11, 1968.

15. *New Haven Journal Courier*, June 4, 1970.

16. Ibid., December 20, 1971.

17. City Demonstration Agency, "Evaluation Comments: Hill Neighborhood Corporation," memorandum, December, 1971.

18. Ibid., p.

19. Hill Neighborhood Corporation, *Report on HNC Performance During the Model Cities First Action Year*, 1971, p. 21.

20. Ibid.

21. Minutes of the City Demonstration Board, February 9, 1972.

22. *New Haven Journal-Courier*, February 26, 1969.

23. *New Haven Register*, November 11, 1971.

24. Ibid., May 23, 1971.

25. Annual Report of Community Progress, Inc., *CPI: The Human Story 1968*, p. 7.

26. Ibid.

27. Ibid.

28. CPI Memorandum, May 12, 1970, p. 1.

29. Report of the West Rock Neighborhood Corporation, 1971.

30. Memorandum to CPI from the Executive Director of the Fairhaven Neighborhood Corporation, October 8, 1970, p. 3.

31. Minutes of United Newhallville Organization, January 19, 1971, p. 2.

32. Services were restricted to "children" under age 21 by the terms of the grant. The daily work of the center was organized around "health teams" made up of a pediatrician, a dentist, two nurses, three community health workers, and a social worker. These teams were "backed up" by supporting services in nutrition, psychiatry, research and education, and health education.

33. A study by the health center of 453 households in the Hill indicated that fewer than 10 percent of the residents "had private physicians to care for either themselves or their children." According to the report, there was a "dearth of physicians and doctors" in the neighborhood "within walking distance." Specifically, in 1968 there were "only 5 local G.P.'s and they basically serve a non-Hill population."

34. As one neighborhood leader put it in 1971, "Yale's game now is to control the Hill Health Center by handpicking the next project director, administrator, and research director," *New Haven Register*. Later the assistant project director resigned charging that Yale controlled the appointments process, *New Haven Register*, June 30, 1971.

35. "A History of Decentralization," *New York Times*, November 29, 1971.

36. Ibid.

37. See Fantini, Gittell, and Magat, and Levine, *Community Control and the Urban School* (New York: Praeger, 1970).

38. *New York Times*, May 23, 1970.

39. According to one report, "It was evident at the meetings that the public, by making its wishes known to the boards, is increasingly seizing on decentralization as a vehicle through which it seeks to influence school policies programs, and the selection of personnel." "Public Using Community Board Meetings to Influence City's Education Policy," *New York Times*, November 25, 1971.

40. See Diane Ravitch, "Community Control Revisited," *Commentary* 4, 53 (February 1972): 74.

41. *New York Daily News*, June 1, 1971.

42. Ibid.

43. The most troubled boards were those in Harlem, East Harlem, the Lower East Side, the Upper West Side and Ocean Hill-Brownsville.

44. Editorial, "School Board Turmoil," *New York Times*, April 26, 1972.

45. Ibid.

46. *New York Times*, November 29, 1971.

47. While precise statistics do not exist on the extent of teacher firings or "reassignments," the minutes of meetings in the ten boards suggest that proceedings against teachers are a rare occurrence. In fact, most of the teachers whose contracts have been terminated were charged with having "abandoned" their duties. On the other hand, by May 1972, eighteen of the thirty-one superintendents had resigned or been fired, many claiming that "political interference" diminished their authority and that "education has become political" (*New York Times*, May 21, 1972).

Another fear was that decentralization would lead to corruption in the administration of school affairs. The evidence is that most boards exhibit some bookkeeping irregularities, but, according to auditors' reports, only a few boards are suspected of repeated malfeasance. Most, but not all of those conflict-ridden boards in the poorest areas have had major auditing problems, as have several boards in middle-income areas. In general, according to school officials, the incidence of suspected misappropriation of funds increases as the income level of the district decreases. Specifically, the widespread irregularities concern the failure of boards to submit "proper receipts" for expenditures and the failure to obtain competitive bids on purchase of supplies and equipment. The most serious irregularities involve the use of school funds for personal ends. In one case, a community board "furnished each of its members with an office in their own homes." In another case, school money was used to buy an expensive suit for a board member. The most common patterns are the use of school money to pay for trips by board members and their families—trips which do not seem to concern school business. These alleged irregularities have generated considerable publicity and have provided new ammunition for adamant critics of decentralization. But again few boards have been implicated in charges of misappropriation, and, in those highly publicized cases, relatively small sums of money were involved. According to the school official responsible for the audit, cash expenditures of $80,000 were considered questionable out of total cash funds of $662,109. (*New York Times*, September 19, 1971).

There is also the fear that nonteaching posts would be filled by patronage appointments. Albert Shanker of the teachers' union has charged that the boards are making a "huge patronage pie out of the school system" and specifically that "about 2,500 people" have been appointed to jobs "for which they were either unqualified or that were created for them." (*New York Times*, May 15, 1972). The evidence of patronage hiring repeats the patterns discussed above. Parent groups in Harlem and Ocean Hill-Brownsville have made charges of "political favoritism" in hiring but the charges have not been proved, and there is no evidence that the practice extends beyond those few, most troubled boards. Board members interviewed speak of "a constant struggle for jobs and about jobs" and recognize that Title I funds provide substantial employment for untrained community people at the paraprofessional level. But most of these board members feel that valid issues are raised in discussions about employment: "who knows the neighborhood, who is committed to improving the schools, who is most sensitive to neighborhood needs?"

48. Since this is an assessment of the direct positive impacts of decentralization, the tests of cost and second order effects are not included.

Notes to Chapter 5 Representation and Internal Democracy

1. For a full discussion of this concept, see Robert Dahl, *Polyarchy* (New Haven: Yale University Press, 1971).

2. See Martin Dworkis, *The Community Planning Boards of New York* (New York: New York University Public Administration Center, 1961).

3. See Robert Merton, "The Latent Functions of the Machine," *Social Theory and Social Structure*, (New York: The Free Press, 1957).

4. Boulton Demas, *The School Elections: A Critique of 1969 New York City School Decentralization*, Report of the Institute for Community Studies, Queens College, 1970, p. 4.

5. Ibid., p. 11.

6. This information was compiled by the Public Education Association and the League of Women Voters.

7. Demas, *School Elections*, p. 24.

8. In Model Cities, where there are three distinct mechanisms for citizen participation, appointment is, on balance, the dominant method of leadership

selection. All the members of the City Demonstration Board and the task forces are appointed, and almost half the board members of the Hill Neighborhood Corporation are appointed (as representatives of major community organizations).

9. See Sar Levitan, *The Great Society's Poor Law* (Baltimore: Johns Hopkins Press, 1969), p. 114.

10. The districts were located in the following low-income areas: the Lower East Side, East and Central Harlem, the South Bronx, the Upper West Side of Manhattan, and the Bedford-Stuyvesant, Fort Greene, and Brownsville areas of Brooklyn.

Notes to Chapter 6
Neighborhood Politicians: Leadership Styles and Political Efficacy

1. This judgment is based on interviews by the author with neighborhood residents and leaders over a two-year period, 1970-72. Similar testimony also appears in the 450 interviews with residents in three New York neighborhoods.

2. These objections and perceptions are summarized in a paper cited above, "Decentralization to Neighborhoods: A Conceptual Analysis," prepared by the staff of the National Advisory Council on Economic Opportunity.

3. See James D. Barber, *The Presidential Character* (Englewood Cliffs, N.J.: Prentice-Hall, 1972), pp. 3-14.

4. See Bell and Held, "The Community Revolution."

5. Barber, *Presidential Character*, p. 6.

6. See Moynihan, *Maximum Feasible Misunderstanding*, p. 129.

7. The evidence on this point is summarized in Robert Lane, *Political Life* (New York: The Free Press, 1959), pp. 152-53.

8. Since every neighborhood leader gave a "yes" answer to at least one question, the range begins with a score of 1 rather than 0 or .5, and thus there are 9 points on the scale.

9. The rhetoric of "participation" and "participatory democracy" implies that participation in any form is a good in itself. This is the meaning of the familiar slogan of the 1960s: "Participation Now." But, as we have seen, participation means many different things, and in some versions, very little as far as political power and control are concerned. For a discussion of the diverse meanings and confusions involved in the concept of participation, see Sherry Arnstein, "A ladder of Citizen Participation," *Journal of the American Institute of Planners* 35 (July 1969): 216-24.

Notes to Chapter 7 The Political Economy of Decentralization

1. For an analysis of the different forms of decentralization, see Chapter 3.

2. This argument was developed in an earlier article. See Douglas Yates, "Neighborhood Government," *Policy Sciences*3 (1972), pp. 209-17. A similar formulation of the costs and beneifts of neighborhood organization is found in Harold Weissman, *Community Councils and Community Control: The Workings of a Democratic Mythology* (Pittsburgh: University of Pittsburgh Press, 1970).

3. For a full discussion of the problems of getting information and bringing it to bear on complex tasks and decisions, see Charles Lindblom, *The Intelligence of Democracy* (New York: Macmillan, 1965).

4. This theme is developed and thoughtfully analyzed in Robert A. Dahl, *After the Revolution* (New Haven: Yale Univèrsity Press, 1971).

5. This argument is supported by William Riker's analysis of "smallest winning coalitions." See William Riker, *The Theory of Political Coalitions* (New Haven: Yale University Press, 1962).

6. For a discussion of the potential for undemocratic behavior in small groups, see Sidney Verba, *Small Groups and Political Behavior*.

7. The term comes from George Washington's Farewell Address.

8. Especially such "skills" as budgeting, accounting, proposal writing ("grantsmanship"), and program education.

9. The concept of political economy has recently taken on a new meaning in addition to the conventional use by economists to describe the economies of the public sector and of public policies. It has been adopted by political scientists to describe an approach that makes use of the language of economic analysis–including cost, benefit, investment, input, and output. For a discussion of the application of these concepts to political analysis, see William C. Mitchell, "The Shape of Political Theory to Come: From Political Sociology to Political Economy," *American Behavioral Scientist* (November-December, 1967), pp. 8-20; L.L. Wade and R.L. Curry, Jr., *A Logic of Public Policy: Aspects of Political Economy* (Belmont, California: Wadsworth Publishing Company, 1970); and Warren Ilchman and Norman Uphoff, *The Political Economy of Change* (Berkeley: University of California Press, 1969). See also a recent article that seeks to apply the concept of political economy to the problems of decentralization: Donald Haider, "The Political Economy of Decentralization," in Smith and La Noue (eds.), "Urban Decentralization and Community Participation" in *American Behavioral Scientist* 15, 1 (Sept./Oct. 1971). Although this article and my chapter make a number of similar points, the perspectives and the analytical frameworks are very different.

10. There are actually several plans for comprehensive neighborhood government in New York. See Heineman and Danzig, "Decentralization in New York City: A Proposal," *Harvard Journal of Legislation*, March 1971, the Lindsay Administration's *Plan for Neighborhood Government* described above, and finally the Task Force on Jurisdiction and Structure of the State Study Commission for New York City, *Restructuring the Government of New York City*, March 1972. The plan for neighborhood government in Minneapolis is contained in Citizens League, *Sub-Urbs in the City* is a report by the Citizens League Committee on Minority Representation in Local Government, May, 1970. A plan for comprehensive decentralization in Boston is found in Harvard Law School, Boston Urban Services Project, *Political and Administrative Decentralization of Municipal Government* in Boston, a report to the Mayor of Boston, 1969.

Notes to Chapter 8 Making Decentralization Work: The View from City Hall

1. For that matter, most of the decentralization experiments we have examined were created by higher-level governments—albeit as a result of political pressure from the neighborhoods. Only the block associations developed independently of government.

2. In 1970, there were Urban Action Task Force offices in twenty-five neighborhoods, and task force activities extended into another twenty neighborhoods. Each task force office had a chairman appointed by the mayor who was also a high-level city official. One or more city employees was assigned to each office to handle citizen complaints and maintain channels of communication with neighborhood groups.

3. See Levine, *Ocean Hill-Brownsville* (New York: Popular Library, 1969), and Fantini, Gittell, and Magat, *Community Control and the Urban School* (New York: Praeger, 1970).

4. With the plans for "command decentralization" and community service cabinets described below.

5. Based on an interview with former Mayor Richard C. Lee of New Haven.

6. This section is based on the author's field work on the Lower East Side conducted as part of a research project for the New York City Rand Institute, Much of this research and analysis has appeared in an internal paper for the Rand Institute: "City Hall and the Neighborhoods: An Analysis of Streetlevel Bureaucracy."

7. It has long been recognized that the location of police stations, fire houses, and schools has important implications for service delivery. For example, police and fire equipment should obviously be located so as to minimize response time (i.e., reduce travel time to all points in the area to be serviced).

Surprisingly, this sensitivity to location has not extended to other government field offices in New York. For neighborhood field offices, even more than fire houses, depend on their location. Unlike fire companies, street-level bureaucrats do not take their services to their clients. Like gas stations or supermarkets, storefronts are fixed; it is assumed that customers will come by to do their shopping or register their complaints. As anyone knows who has ever set up a gas station, it makes all the difference where it is located. The central principle of location is to maximize coverage of the areas in which one seeks to draw clients, and, for this reason, the commercial entrepreneur will seek out a highly visible and heavily traveled location.

Analyzing the location of government field offices on the Lower East Side, it is clear that public entrepreneurs would make poor gas station owners. Government offices were often located on side streets, and, more important, they were hard to identify. In the case of the Mayor's Urban Task Force Office, a small sign in the window was the only visible identification. Other task force offices revealed this same almost studied anonymity. In east Harlem, the office was located in a second story room and had no identifying signs at all. With gas stations, at least one can always spot gas pumps. With the task force office, the citizen has to search for the office in order to find it.

In terms of coverage, it seems obvious that government offices would be convenient to more people if they were distributed around the neighborhood. But on the Lower East Side, government offices as well as community organizations were concentrated in one place (around Third Street between Avenues B and C).

8. Of course, block lengths differ throughout the city, but the marginal differences should not greatly affect the conclusions.

9. I would grant that this recognition test is open to question on methodological grounds. Some people might simply not have wanted to waste time and information on a stranger. Puerto Ricans might not have understood me although I spoke in Spanish with some. I guarded against these problems by only counting interviews in which residents had been willing to talk with me for a minute or so and in which further questioning proved that they were able to understand what I was saying.

10. This survey was conducted jointly by the author and the Office of Neighborhood Government.

11. Internal Memorandum, Office of Neighborhood Government, 1971.

12. Ibid.

13. This judgment is based on two analyses of administrative coordination and decentralization in city departments by the Office of Neighborhood Government (ONG). The first is a summary and analysis of communications between ONG and city departments on the prospects for, and the problems of, administrative decentralization. See Office of Neighborhood Government, "Administrator's Replies and Analyses," October 21, 1971. See also an analysis

by a staff member of ONG and two business school students on the same subject: Office of Neighborhood Government, *E Unum Pluribus: A Managerial Analysis of Command Decentralization in New York Superagencies*, May 9, 1972.

14. These interviews were also conducted jointly by the author and the Office of Neighborhood Government.

15. See Wilson, *Varieties of Police Behavior*, p. 6, and Lipsky, "Toward a Theory of Streetlevel Bureaucracy."

16. Mayor John V. Lindsay, *Program for the Decentralized Administration of Municipal Services in New York City Communities*, December 1971, p. 1.

Notes to Chapter 9
The Future of Neighborhood Government: Consensus and Conflict

1. This survey was made jointly by the author and the Office of Neighborhood Government in New York. Interviews were conducted by student interviewers in the winter months of 1971-72. The technique used in interviewing was area sampling.

2. Unless otherwise noted, all direct quotations in this chapter are from interviews by the author or from the files of the consultations conducted by the Office of Neighborhood Government, New York City.

3. This finding is based on the interviews with sixty neighborhood public employees described in Chapter 8.

4. Memorandum to the mayor from Lewis Feldstein, Office of Neighborhood Government, "Report on the Consultations on the Plan for Neighborhood Government," undated, p. 1.

5. Ibid.

6. In order to make the scoring reflect the distribution of opinion as closely as possible, two points were scored when a theme appeared in a letter from a community or political organization, one point in a letter from an individual. However, most of the "position papers" in the consultation file were submitted by organizations.

7. See Percy Sutton, Borough President of Manhattan, *A Plan for Localized Government for New York City*, February 1972 and Robert Abrams, Borough President of the Bronx, *A Plan for Borough and Neighborhood Government in New York City*, May 1970.

8. From the files of the Office of Neighborhood Government.

9. Although generalizations from New York's experience cannot be validly applied to other cities, there is good reason to believe that the same social and organizational sources of resistance would exist in other cities. Also, many other cities have had the same frustrating experience with experimental urban

programs, and we would therefore expect that the same suspiciousness and cynicism would be found among neighborhood residents in other large cities.

Notes to Chapter 10
Decentralization, Development, and Democracy

1. That is, we can hardly expect the Community Task Force to serve as a neighborhood forum or assembly or the community school board members to be active grassroots organizers. Constraints of time, task, and temperament preclude it.

2. Particularly relevant is the experience of block associations, community boards, neighborhood corporations, and community school boards that exist in different neighborhoods. The predictions presented here are based on the variations we have found in the way that the impact of each experiment varies from neighborhood to neighborhood.

3. See Leonard Binder et al., *Crises and Sequences in Political Development* (Princeton: Princeton University Press, 1971).

4. Ibid., p. 31.

5. According to Lucian Pye, "In the process of political development an identity crisis occurs when a community finds that what it had once accepted as the physical and psychological definitions of its collective self are no longer acceptable . . . in order for the political system to reach a new level of performance, it is necessary for the participants to redefine who they are and how they are different from all other political and social systems." Pye, "Identity and the Political Culture," in Binder, *Crises and Sequences*, pp. 110-111.

6. See Lipsky, *Protest in City Politics*.

7. This judgment is based on an analysis of six New Haven community leaders who were prominent in the late 1960s.

8. For a full discussion of this phenomenon see Moynihan, *Maximum Feasible Participation*.

9. See Albert O. Hirschman, *The Strategy of Economic Development* (New Haven: Yale University Press, 1958), pp. 62-75.

10. David E. Apter, *Choice and the Politics of Allocation* (New Haven: Yale University Press, 1971), p. 7 ff.

11. See Charles E. Lindblom, *The Intelligence of Democracy* (New York: Free Press, 1965).

12. This is also the title of a very useful book: Mancur Olson, Jr., *The Logic of Collective Action* (Cambridge: Harvard University Press, 1968).

13. Ibid., pp. 53-65.

14. See Donald T. Campbell, "Reforms As Experiments," *American Psychologist* 24 (April 1969): 409-429.

15. See Albert Hirschman, *Exit, Voice, and Loyalty* (Cambridge: Harvard University Press, 1970), pp. 120-26.

16. See, for example, Altshuler, *Community Control* (New York: Pegasus, 1970), Kotler, *Neighborhood Government*, (New York: Bobbs-Merrill, 1969), and Robert Dahl, "The City in the Future of Democracy," *American Political Science Review* 61 (December 1967): 953-70, presidential address.

17. This view is presented forcefully in Theodore Lowi, *The End of Liberalism* (New York: Norton, 1969), pp. 191-214.

Bibliography

Bibliography

A Selected Bibliography

The published material on citizen participation is by now voluminous. I will not attempt to reproduce it here. For general inventory see Judith May, "Citizen Participation: A Review of the Literature, Council of Planning Libraries, Exchange Bibliography #210-211" (August 1971). Instead, I list below the books and articles that were most useful to me organized around the main topics of concern.

A. The Urban Neighborhood

Gans, Herbert. *The Urban Villagers*. New York: The Free Press, 1962.

Gist, Noel, and Fava, Sylvia. *Urban Society*. New York: Crowell, 1964, 5th ed.

Hannerz, Ulf. *Soulside: Inquiries into Ghetto Culture and Community*. New York: Columbia University Press, 1969.

Keller, Susanne. *The Urban Neighborhood*. New York: Random House, 1968.

Keyes, Langley, C. *The Rehabilitation Planning Game: A Study in the Diversity of Neighborhood*. Cambridge: MIT Press, 1969.

Liebow, Elliot. *Tally's Corner*. Boston: Little Brown, 1967.

Park, Robert; Burgess, Ernest; and McKenzie, Roderick. *The City*. Chicago: University of Chicago Press, 1923.

Suttles, Gerald. *The Social Order of the Slum*. Chicago: University of Chicago Press, 1968.

Warren, Roland. *The Community in America*. Chicago: Rand McNally, 1963.

B. The Structure of Urban Government

Banfield, Edward. *Political Influence*. New York: The Free Press, 1961.

Banfield, Edward, and Wilson, James Q. *City Politics*. Cambridge: Harvard University Press, 1965.

Dahl, Robert A. *Who Governs?* New Haven: Yale University Press, 1961.

Lineberry, Robert, and Sharkansky, Ira. *Urban Politics and Public Policy*. New York: Harper and Row, 1971.

Rogers, David. *110 Livingston Street*. New York: Vintage, 1968.

Sayre, Wallace, and Kaufman, Herbert. *Governing New York City*. New York: Russell Sage Foundation, 1965.

C. Historical Perspectives on Decentralization

Callow, Alexander B. Jr. (ed.). *American Urban History*. New York: Oxford University Press, 1969.
Dahir, James. *The Neighborhood Unit Plan–Its Spread and Acceptance*. New York: Russell Sage Foundation, 1947.
Glaab, Charles, and Brown, A. Theodore. *A History of Urban America*. New York: Macmillan, 1967.
Griffith, Ernest. *History of American City Government: The Colonial Period*. New York: Oxford University Press, 1936.
Griffith, Ernest. *Modern Development of City Government*. London, Oxford University Press, 1927, 2 vols.
Mandelbaum, Seymour. *Boss Tweed's New York*. New York: Wiley, 1965.
Mumford, Lewis. *The Urban Prospect*. London: Secken and Warburg, 1968.
Mushkat, Jerome. *Tammany: The Evolution of a Political Machine. 1789-1865*. Syracuse: Syracuse University Press, 1971.
Syed, Anwar. *The Political Theory of American Local Government*. New York: Random House, 1966.
White, Morton, and White, Lucia. *The Intellectual Versus the City*. Cambridge: Harvard University Press, 1962.
Zink, Harold. *City Bosses in the United States*. Durham, North Carolina: Duke University Press, 1930.

E. The Decentralization Debate

Advisory Commission on Intergovernmental Relations. *Neighborhood Subunits of Government*. Washington, D.C.: U.S. Government Printing Office, 1970.
Altshuler, Alan. *Community Control*. New York: Pegasus, 1970.
Association of the Bar. "A Discussion Draft: For a Symposium on Decentralizing New York City Government." New York: Association of the Bar of the City of New York, 1970.
Committee for Economic Development. *Reshaping Government in Metropolitan Areas*. New York: Committee for Economic Development, 1970.
Kaufman, Herbert. "Administrative Decentralization and Political Power," *Public Administration Review* 29 (January-February 1969).
Kotler, Milton. *Neighborhood Government*. New York: Bobbs-Merrill, 1969.
Kotler, Milton. "Two Essays on the Neighborhood Corporation," in *Urban America: Goals and Problems*. Washington, D.C.: Joint Economic Committee, 1967.
Kristol, Irving. "Decentralization for What," *The Public Interest*, No. 11 (Spring 1968).
Levin, Henry (ed.). *Community Control of Schools*. New York: Simon and Schuster, 1970.

National Advisory Council on Economic Opportunity. "Decentralization to Neighborhoods." Internal staff paper, 1970.

Smith, Bruce, and La Noue, George. "Urban Decentralization and Community Participation," *American Behavioral Scientist* 15 (September-October 1971).

D. The Background of Citizen Participation

Bell, Daniel, and Held, Virginia. "The Community Revolution," *The Public Interest* 16 (Summer 1969).

Berube, Maurice, and Gittel, Marilyn (eds.). *Confrontation at Ocean Hill-Brownsville*. New York: Praeger, 1969.

Bloomberg, Warren, and Schmandt, Harry (eds.). *Power, Poverty, and Urban Policy*. Beverly Hills: Sage Publications, 1968.

Donovan, John C. *The Politics of Poverty*. New York: Pegasus, 1967.

Gittell, Marilyn. *Participants and Participation*. New York: Praeger, 1967.

Kramer, Ralph. *Participation of the Poor*. Englewood Cliffs, N.J.: Prentice-Hall, 1969.

Levitan, Sar. *The Great Society's Poor Law*. Baltimore: Johns Hopkins Press, 1969.

Lipsky, Michael. *Protest in City Politics*. Chicago: Rand McNally, 1970.

Marris, Peter, and Rein, Martin. *Dilemmas of Social Reform*. New York: Atherton Press, 1967.

Miller, S.M., and Rein, Martin. "Participation, Poverty and Administration," *Public Administration Review* 29 (January-February 1969).

Mogulof, Melvin. "Coalition to Adversary: Citizen Participation in Three Federal Programs," *Journal of the American Institute of Planners* 35 (July 1969).

Moynihan, Daniel P. *Maximum Feasible Misunderstanding*. New York: The Free Press, 1969.

Office of Economic Opportunity. *Community Action Program Guide*. Washington, D.C.: OEO, 1965.

Sundquist, James L. *On Fighting Poverty: Perspectives From Experience*. New York: Basic Books, 1969.

Wilson, James Q. "Planning and Politics: Citizen Participation in Urban Renewal." *Journal of the American Institute of Planners* Vol. 29, No. 4 (November, 1963).

F. Current Experiments in Decentralization

Bureau of Municipal Research. "Neighborhood Participation in Local Government," *Civic Affairs* 6 (January 1970).

Cahn, Edgar, and Passett, Barry (eds.) *Citizen Participation*. Trenton, New Jersey: New Jersey Community Action Training Institute, 1969.

Center for Governmental Studies, Conference Proceedings, *Public Administration and Neighborhood Control*. Washington, D.C., May 1970.

Cunningham, James. *The Resurgent Neighborhood*. Notre Dame, Indiana: Fides Publishers, 1965.

Fantini, Mario; Gittell, Marilyn; and Magat, Richard. *Community Control and the Urban School*. New York: Praeger, 1970.

Frederickson, H. George (ed.). *Politics, Public Administration, and Neighborhood Control*. San Francisco: Chandler, 1971.

Haddad, William, and Pugh, G. Douglas (eds.). *Black Economic Development*. Englewood Cliffs, New Jersey: Prentice-Hall, 1909.

Hallman, Howard. *Neighborhood Control of Public Programs*. New York: Praeger, 1970.

Hallman, Howard. *Community Corporations and Neighborhood Control*. Washington, D.C.: Center for Governmental Studies, 1970.

Herzog, Barry, "Participation by the Poor in Federal Health Programs," *Wisconsin Law Review* (November 3, 1970).

Kahn, Alfred J. *Neighborhood Information Centers*. New York: Columbus University School of Social Work. 1966.

Nordlinger, Eric. "Decentralizing the American City: A Case Study of Boston's Little City Halls." Unpublished manuscript.

Powledge, Fred. *Model City*. New York: Simon and Schuster, 1970.

Spiegel, Hans, and Mittenthal, Stephen. *Neighborhood Power and Control*. New York: Institute of Urban Environment, School of Architecture, Columbus University, 1968.

Warren, Roland L. "Model Cities First Round: Politics, Planning, and Participation." *Journal of the American Institute of Planners* 35 (July 1969).

Washnis, George. *Neighborhood Facilities and Municipal Decentralization*. Washington, D.C.: Center for Governmental Studies, 1971, Vols. I and II.

Weissman, Harold. *Community Councils and Community Control: The Workings of a Democratic Mythology*. Pittsburgh: University of Pittsburgh Press, 1970.

G. Decentralization in Political Systems

Arnstein, Sherry. "A Ladder of Citizen Participation." *Journal of the American Institute of Planners* 35 (July 1969).

Black, Guy. *The Decentralization of Urban Government: A Systems Approach*. Staff Discussion Paper 102, Program of Policy Studies in Science and Technology. Washington, D.C.: George Washington University, 1968.

Codding, George A. *The Federal Government of Switzerland*. Boston: Houghton Mifflin, 1901.

Fesler, James W. "Approaches to the Study of Decentralization." *Journal of Politics* 27 (1965).

Fesler, James W. (ed.). *The 50 States and Their Local Governments*. New York: Knopf, 1967.
Maass, Arthur (ed.). *Area and Power: A Theory of Local Government*. Glencoe, Illinois' The Free Press, 1959.
Selznick, Phillip. *TVA and the Grass Roots*. Berkeley: University of California Press, 1949.
Sundquist, James L. *Making Federalism Work*. Washington, D.C.: The Brookings Institution, 1969.
Vile, M.J.C. *The Structure of American Federalism*. Oxford: Oxford University Press, 1961.
Walsh, Ann Marie Hauck. *The Urban Challenge to Government*. New York: Praeger, 1969.
Wildavsky, Aaron (ed.). *American Federalism in Perspective*. Boston, Little Brown, 1967.

H. Political Leadership

Barber, James David. *The Lawmakers*. New Haven: Yale University Press, 1965.
Barber, James David. *Power in Committees: An Experiment in the Governmental Process*. Chicago: Rand McNally, 1966.
Barber, James David. *The Presidential Character*. Englewood Cliffs, N.J.: Prentice-Hall, 1972.
Edinger, Lewis (ed.). *Political Leadership in Industrialized Societies*. New York: Wiley, 1967.
Frohlich, Norman; Oppenheimer, Joe; and Young, Oran. *Political Leadership and Collective Goods*. Princeton: Princeton University Press, 1971.
Greenstein, Fred I. *Personality and Politics*. Chicago: Markham, 1969.
Lane, Robert E. *Political Life*. New York: The Free Press, 1959.
Lane, Robert E. *Political Ideology*. New York: The Free Press, 1962.
McFarland, Andrew S. *Power and Leadership in Pluralist Systems*. Stanford: Stanford University Press, 1969.
Wilson, James Q. *Negro Politics: The Search for Leadership*. New York: The Free Press, 1960.

I. The Concept of Political Economy

Curry, R.L., Jr., and Wade, L.L. *A Theory of Political Exchange*. Englewood Cliffs, N.J.: Prentice-Hall, 1968.
Ilchman, Warren F., and Uphoff, Norman T. *The Political Economy of Change*. Berkeley: University of California Press, 1969.
Mitchell, William C. "The Shape of Political Theory to Come: From Political

Sociology to Political Economy." *American Behavioral Scientist* 11 (November-December 1967).

Mitchell, William C. "The New Political Economy." *Social Research* 35 (Spring 1968).

Wade, L.L. and Curry, R.L., Jr. *A Logic of Public Policy: Aspects of Political Economy*. Belmont, California: Wadsworth, 1970.

J. The Analysis of Public Policy

Allison, Graham. *Essence of Decision*. Boston: Little, Brown, 1971.

Bauer, Raymond and Gergen, Kenneth (eds.). *The Study of Policy Formation*. New York: The Free Press, 1968.

Braybrooke, David and Lindblom, Charles E. *A Strategy of Decision: Policy Evaluation as a Social Process*. New York: The Free Press, 1963.

Dror, Yehezkel. *Public Policymaking Reexamined*. San Francisco: Chandler, 1968.

Dye, Thomas R. *Understanding Public Policy*. Englewood Cliffs, N.J.: Prentice-Hall, 1972.

Havemen, Robert, and Margolis, Julius. *Public Expenditures and Policy Analysis*. Chicago: Markham, 1970.

Lowi, Theodore. "American Business, Public Policy, Case-Studies, and Political Theory." *World Politics* 16 (July 1964).

Ranney, Austin (ed.). *Political Science and Public Policy*. Chicago: Markham, 1968.

Sharkansky, Ira (ed.). *Policy Analysis in Political Science*. Chicago: Markham.

K. Decentralization and Development

Almond, Gabriel, and Verba, Sidney. *The Civic Culture: Political Attitudes and Democracy in Five Nations*. Princeton: Princeton University Press, 1960.

Apter, David E. *Choice and the Politics of Allocation*. New Haven: Yale University Press, 1971.

Apter, David E. *Some Conceptual Approaches to the Study of Modernization*. Englewood Cliffs, N.J.: Prentice-Hall, 1968.

Apter, David E. *The Politics of Modernization*. Chicago: University of Chicago Press, 1965.

Black, C.E. *The Dynamics of Modernization*. New York: Harper and Row, 1966.

Binder, Leonard et al. *Crises and Sequences in Political Development*. Princeton, New Jersey: Princeton University Press, 1971.

Clinard, Marshall B. *Slums and Community Development*. New York: The Free Press, 1966.

Hirschman, Albert O. *Exit, Voice, and Loyalty*. Cambridge: Harvard University Press, 1970.

Hirschman, Albert O. *The Strategy of Economic Development*. New Haven: Yale University Press, 1958.

La Palombara, Joseph (ed.). *Bureaucracy and Political Development*. Princeton: Princeton University Press, 1963.

Lindblom, Charles E. *The Intelligence of Democracy*. New York: The Free Press, 1965.

Lowi, Theodore J. *The Politics of Disorder*. New York: Basic Books, 1971.

Lowi, Theodore. *The End of Liberalism*. New York: Norton, 1969.

Olson, Mancur, Jr. *The Logic of Collective Action*. Cambridge: Harvard University Press, 1968.

Pye, Lucian W. *Aspects of Political Development*. Boston: Little Brown, 1960.

Warren, Roland L. (ed.). *Politics and the Ghettoes*. New York: Atherton Press, 1969.

L. Decentralization and Democracy

Barry, Brian. *Political Argument*. London: Routledge and Kegan Paul, 1965.

Braybrooke, David. *Three Tests For Democracy: Personal Rights, Human Welfare, Collective Preference*. New York: Random House, 1968.

Dahl, Robert A. *Polyarchy: Participation and Opposition*. New Haven: Yale University Press, 1971.

Dahl, Robert A. *After the Revolution?* New Haven: Yale University Press, 1970.

Dahl, Robert A. "The City in the Future of Democracy." *American Political Science Review* 61 (December 1967).

Dahl, Robert A. *A Preface to Democratic Theory*. Chicago: University of Chicago Press, 1956.

Minar, David, and Greer, Scott. *The Concept of Community*. Chicago: Aldine, 1969.

Nisbet, Robert. *Community and Power*. New York: Oxford University Press, 1962.

Pitkin, Hanna. *The Concept of Representation*. Berkeley: University of California Press, 1967.

Spiro, Herbert. *Responsibility in Government: Theory and Practice*. New York: Von Nostrand Reinhold, 1969.

Index

Index

About the Author

Douglas Yates is an Assistant Professor at Yale University. He is also Assistant to the Director of Yale's Institution for Social and Policy Studies. A graduate of Yale, Mr. Yates attended Balliol College, Oxford as a Rhodes Scholar and received the Ph.D. from Yale in 1972. He is a consultant to the New York City Rand Institute and has worked for the City of New York and the State of Connecticut's Department of Community Affairs.